Eskimo Poems
from Canada and Greenland

Translated by
TOM LOWENSTEIN

from material originally collected by
KNUD RASMUSSEN

Allison & Busby
London

First published in 1973 by
Allison & Busby Limited, 6a Noel Street, London W1V 3RB

English translations of poems © 1973 Tom Lowenstein

SBN 85031 076 8 (hardback)

SBN 85031 110 1 (paperback)

ACKNOWLEDGEMENTS are due to Knud Rasmussen's
executors, Rudolf Sand & William Bentzen, for permission
to translate his work, and to his publishers Gyldendalske
Boghandel of Copenhagen.
   Some of these translations have already appeared in
*The Chelsea Review, The Chicago Review, The Poetry Review,
Telephone,* and *The World.*

PRINTED IN GREAT BRITAIN BY THE ANCHOR PRESS LTD,
AND BOUND BY WM. BRENDON & SON LTD, BOTH OF
TIPTREE, ESSEX

Contents

II: HUNTING SONGS

III: SONGS OF DERISION

IV: CHARMS

Preface

Snehyttens Sange (literally, "Songs from the Snow-hut") consists of the songs Knud Rasmussen selected from the larger body of material that he gathered over the first quarter of this century in Canada and Greenland. All the Canadian songs can be found scattered through Volumes 7, 8, and 9 of the *Report of the Fifth Thule Expedition*, which was published by Gyldendal (Copenhagen) between 1927 and 1930, in Danish and also in English translations by W. E. Calvert and W. Worster. The Greenland material comes from Volumes 1 and 3 of *Myter og Sagn fra Groenland* ("Myths and Legends from Greenland"), Gyldendal, 1921. None of the songs from the latter source have previously been translated into English. To the original format of *Snehyttens Sange* (which consisted of the songs in the present book, with Rasmussen's Afterword), I have added extracts from the *Report of the Fifth Thule Expedition* to serve as notes. A few of the shorter notes are my own—based largely on Rasmussen's material.

Some of Calvert's and Worster's versions of the songs have been previously anthologised or re-shaped:[1] but, as far as I know, this is the first time Rasmussen's Danish has been translated since 1930. It should be emphasised here that the translations in this book are only from Rasmussen's Danish, and were made in collaboration with Ida Lowenstein.

The only other extensive collections of Eskimo songs that exist to my knowledge are *Eskimo Songs* (*Songs of the Copper*

[1] Edmund Carpenter, *Anerca* (J. M. Dent, Canada, 1959); Jerome Rothenberg, *Technicians of the Sacred* (Doubleday, New York, 1968).

ix

Eskimos),[1] collected by D. Jenness between 1913 and 1918, and *Poèmes Esquimax*,[2] collected by Paul-Emile Victor in the 1930s.

While the flavour of Victor's versions is extremely French, Jenness's *Eskimo Songs* contains 137 pieces, with their melodies, printed both in Eskimo and in literal English translations. However, the quality of these versions differs from those of Rasmussen in several ways. As Jenness himself points out in the Introduction to *Songs of the Copper Eskimos*, his knowledge of the Eskimo language was insufficient, and he found the content of the songs obscure, very often, as he points out, a result of their being perpetually carried from community to community, and undergoing modification in the process :

For all these reasons it is only to be expected that a large proportion of the dance-songs are virtually unintelligible. All the individual words—except, of course, the burden syllables —may be capable of translation, yet taken together they will yield no meaning. To the Eskimo this matters little; his main requirement, whether for singing or dancing, is the tune, and he can often be satisfied with burden syllables alone. A newly composed song may be hardly more intelligible than one that has travelled a long distance. All that the first audience needs are a few catch-words, since the composer is sure to give an explanation in a short speech. Songs of this character, when transmitted to other communities without the explanation, as so often happens, become quite meaningless; an example is No. 53, which was learned by its Piuvliq singer from a Prince Albert Sound native in the summer of 1915. There are cases probably where the obscurity lies in the translation rather than in the original, owing to my imperfect knowledge of the language and in inadequacy of my interpreter; but in the majority of instances the songs themselves are at fault, from one or more of the causes that have been outlined above.

Although he presents the song as anthropological data rather than as poetry, many of the literal versions Jenness made

---

[1] *Report of the Canadian Arctic Expedition 1913–18*, Volume XIV, by Helen Roberts and D. Jenness (Ottawa, 1925).

[2] Seghers, Paris, 1959. Both in *Poèmes Esquimaux* and in *My Eskimo Life* (Simon and Schuster, New York, 1939), Victor alludes to over 800 songs he collected in Eastern Greenland. *Poèmes Esquimaux* contains 17 pieces.

are very beautiful, and the fragments, too, should not be "found at fault":

No. 53

Seeing that I was longing for it,
I gave it a name, the spirit.

Much blood pours from me (my nose) unexpectedly.
I gave it a name, seeing that I recognised it.

I have not finished it (my song) however.
Whither my little sister, my little *Kaniraq* (has she gone).

Much blood pours from me unexpectedly.
Whither my little sister—I have not finished it however.[1]

No. 85
? falling tears,
? falling tears,
The old knee down there,
The old knee down there,
It splashes on it, it splashes on it.

No. 104
My great companion, my great guardian spirit,
My great companion, my great guardian spirit.
Our fine incantation, our fine cries.
There is no snow-hut; it is empty of people.
He is not a real man; it is empty of people.
Underneath it down there let us two search.

In the comments I have quoted from Jenness, there is a tendency to attribute the obscurities of the songs largely to social causes, and to judge them by European standards of coherency rather than in their own terms. In contrast, Rasmussen's interest in the songs was very much more than anthropological.

[1] The words are said to be taken from three different songs.

Fragmentary and difficult as he found much of the material he collected, he took its validity for granted, as did the Eskimos themselves, to whom literal "coherent" meaning was not always a quality determining a poem's worth. Rather than censure the discontinuities, Rasmussen acknowledged that the attributes of brevity and concentration which initially made comprehension impossible were highly regarded poetic devices, which only a very good singer was capable of. Many of the songs that Jenness found at fault may have been as deliberately elliptical as, for example, the original versions of *Reindeer* in the Rasmussen collection. In conclusion to his discussion of Aua's composition of that song (see notes, pp. 134–7), Rasmussen sums up:

Of course it is by no means all songs that are abbreviated in the text. It is done occasionally, because this also is reckoned to be something of a gift, to be able to convey the essence of a great event by the slightest indication. Finally, there is also the self-consciousness of the great hunter, underlying the view that one's adventures are so generally known that there is no need to describe them in detail. Accompanied by the weird rumble of the drum, one then flings out now and again, between repetitions of the stirring aja ja, such simple words as:

"All unexpected I came and took by surprise the heedless!"

The voice is raised and lowered in accord with the melody:

"All unexpected I came and took by surprise the heedless!'

The dancer and singer suits the movements of his body to the steadily increasing force of the chorus:

"All unexpected I came and took by surprise the heedless!"

And at last all believe they are themselves taking part in the happenings described.

Rasmussen's acount of the evolution of Aua's hunting songs forces on our attention the disparity of the two cultures that he fuses in his translations. Some readers might be tempted to dismiss his freer versions as semi-colonialist violations of the source-material. On the other hand, the accounts of conversations with singers that Rasmussen provides us with suggest that he was well aware of the dangers of distortion, and also that he went to inordinate lengths, both in the field and in his translations, to transcribe the songs faithfully and communicate as much as would ever be possible of them to European readers. And that his unique combination of qualifications made him an ideal translator is borne out by the fact that, unfortunately, no other Eskimologist has been able to do the same, in spite of abundant material.

It is a tragedy that so much of the Eskimo song-culture has been lost; but it is also something of a miracle that Rasmussen was there to collect before it was too late. We owe the survival of the songs we have, in the clear form in which he rendered them, to the balance he maintained between his functions as anthropologist and poet. As an anthropologist, he avoided collecting the songs merely as factual data; and as a writer, eschewed doing a Walter Scott job on them. In both capacities, it was his concern, and in his interest, to present the songs in as pure a form as he could. Obviously, in choosing his material for *Snehyttens Sange*, he selected the songs that would translate into the best Danish. This was a courtesy both to the Eskimo singers and the Danish audience: he did not have a recondite following in mind, and as translators we share his hope that the songs will reach a wide and varied readership.

Introduction

In editing the notes to the poems, my motive was partly to provide some idea of their context, but it was also to indicate the individuality of the singers. Possibly as a result of current interest in ethnic poetry, there is a tendency to think in terms of cultures, at the expense of the individual artists within them. It would be a pity if, putting down this book, the reader should only be conscious of having read some Eskimo poems and not, specifically, the songs of Kibkarjuk, Uvavnuk, Orpingalik, Tatilgak, Netsit, etc.—all of whom seemed to have raised the language of individual expression to a pitch of remarkable intensity.

In any anthology there is a danger of reifying poets into categories, and there is a particular danger of this when it comes to the poetry of so-called primitive people. One of Rasmussen's unusual qualities as an anthropologist was his interest in people, as well as in *the* people. Since he was a Greenlander himself, his work among the Eskimos involved association and identification as well as pure research into ''the other''. Not only did this enable him to distinguish between individual and group characteristics, but he saw the group largely through the experience of individuals, rather than merely by means of information they provided. As a result of this, he is able to give us a picture of Eskimo song that does not just add up to a generalised aspect of a homogeneous folk-culture, where the singer subordinated his style and subject-matter to the norms of the group. The group norms were manifestly there but, rather than determining what should be sung, they provided opportunities and encouragement for individual expression.

Of course, the common environment and the available range of experience limited the variety of subjects that could be used in song: but even in the hunting songs the theme is almost always dealt with in its particulars, and in response to fresh personal experience. Moreover, the forms built into the culture which the singer could exploit were very loose. For example, the songs of derision and the two-part form the Copper Eskimos used (see note p. 116) were altogether open for the poet's inspirational handling, and in most cases the received structure gets lost in that of the singer. The struggle to create form was therefore largely the poet's own responsibility: an imperative which was keenly and often crushingly felt, as is indicated by the frequent allusions to the difficulties of composition and a fear of failure—failure to perfect the song itself, and then to perform it in the feasting-house without forgetting the words:

> It's wonderful to make up songs,
> but all too many of them fail . . .
> (Piuvkaq, *Delight in Singing*)

And in another song, which is part of a sequence not included in this volume, Piuvkaq continues:

> I recognise what I want to put into words,
> but it does not come well-arranged,
> it does not become worth listening to.
> Something that is well-arranged,
> something well worth hearing
> hastily to put *that* together
> *that* is often difficult.
> An awkward one—maybe so—I have put together.
>> (*Report of the Fifth Thule Expedition*, Vol. 8,
>> part 2)

A successful song, then, is one that is "worth listening to", so a singer's feeling about his work is often expressed as an anxiety that he will bungle the performance in the *quagsé* (the feasting-house where the songs were publicly performed), that he will forget the *words* when the moment comes to sing:

> It was always hard
> to join the happy company
> that sang in the feasting-house:
> for I could never remember
> the words of my little song
> in the drum-dance . . .
> (Qerraq, *Song of a Diffident Man*)

> Life was wonderful
> when you danced in the feasting-house;
> but did this make me any happier?
> No, I always worried
> I'd forget my song . . .
> (Netsit, *Dead Man's Song*)

It is significant that in the whole complex activity of performance—i.e. simultaneous singing, dancing, drumming and "conducting"—it is to the words that the anxiety, and therefore the greatest importance, is attached. There are no songs expressive of despair about the drumming or the dance, or failure to bring in the chorus properly. The words were always at the root of the anxiety. Forgetting the words, in a culture without paper, would be like losing the song. No one would be there to prompt. It would be as if the words no longer existed at all, even though, in an earlier, private stage of its evolution, the song had been painstakingly memorised. In the feasting-house performance, the word was the only one among the other cultural variables (costumes, dancing, drumming, refrains) that was not a shared and indestructible certainty. It was almost as if the words had a life of their own, the power of whose presence, or the gap left by whose absence, confirmed or threatened the very being of the singer.

This relationship between language and life itself is suggested by the Eskimo word *anerca*, with its double meaning of breath and poetry. As Orpingalik says about his death-bed song: "This is what I call my song because it is as important to me to sing it as it is to draw breath." The hard-won strength of the finished song, with its often elusive but essentially life-giving qualities, remains very much a part of the singer's private experience: it is only at that moment when the singer adds to it the drumming and the dance, and brings the as yet uninitiated chorus-audience into participation, that the compositional process blends with the general culture. The new becomes familiar—though, as a rule, the song remains the poet's property, and no one else is entitled to sing it.

It will be noticed, however, that there are no songs that concern themselves exclusively with composition. All of them weave it into their treatment of practical matters, such as hunting and survival. *Delight in Singing,* for example (see p. 45), proceeds from the subject of singing to that of hunting:

> It's wonderful
> to hunt reindeer,
> but all too seldom
> one succeeds,
> standing like a bright fire
> over the plain.

In *Dead Man's Song* (p. 10), the first three verses of the second section are about the problems of getting enough hides for clothing and bed-wear, etc. Similarly, in *Song of a Diffident Man,* Qerraq compares his incompetence as a hunter with other men's success. And at the end of the poem (quoted on p. xvii) he comes to the problem of remembering his song in the feasting-house. Finally, Ikinilik, an old man of the Utku-hikjalik Folk, who partly out of listlessness no longer catches all the fish he needs, concludes his song:

For I'm just an ordinary hunter,
who never inherited singing
from the bird-song of the sky.

It will be noticed that ideas surrounding the process of com-
position coincide at some points with those about hunting:
a man's survival, his self-esteem and his reputation all hang on
his skill as a hunter. In the latter two cases, the same could be
said of him in his singer's role. This isn't to suggest that the
two activities were of equal importance: it would be impossible
to measure this, and one might too easily arrive at an over-
sentimental or too hard-headed conclusion. But the two activi-
ties were parallel in their effect, both for what they meant to the
individual and in the amount of soul and skill that went into
either pursuit. To be sure, both hunting and composition were
attended by a certain mystery (hunting was controlled univer-
sally by a system of taboos, and singing, an equally everday
pursuit, was also somehow charmed, as Kilimé says: "We do
not know how songs arrive with our breath, in the form of
words and music and not as ordinary speech . . ."), but the
Eskimos could hardly have survived had they relied on their
spells and not developed a hunting-technology; nor would their
songs have attained such sophistication had they depended on
their spirits to make them up for shamans in moments of un-
predictable inspiration. Just as the physical life of the group was
sustained by survival-techniques, so it was a craft and discipline
in song-composition that brought the poetry into existence. A
conscious application of skill was as necessary for the com-
position of a successful song as a knowledge of sealing tech-
niques was to the same man in his capacity as a hunter.

Rasmussen gives us several vivid pictures of the laborious
and self-conscious process that composition was. Vatic exuber-
ance like the shaman Uvavnuk's certainly existed (see note p.
125), and non-shamans would also burst spontaneously into song
—like the Iglulik woman Takornaq, in the middle of relating
her autobiography:

At this point in Takornaq's story the meat in the pot began
to boil, and she interrupted her narration to serve up a meal.
Tea was made from our own supply, and the old woman was so
pleased at this little trivial courtesy that she at once improvised
a song, the words of which were as follows :

Ajaja—aja—jaja,
The lands around my dwelling
Are more beautiful
From the day
When it is given me to see
Faces I have never seen before.
All is more beautiful,
All is more beautiful,
And life is thankfulness.
These guests of mine
Make my house grand,
Ajaja—aja—jaja.

But in most cases, a quasi-Wordsworthian process took place,
in which the poet retired into the solitude of nature, and
struggled to fit words to the tune he had previously composed.
The struggle, like that of any poet, was hopefully relieved by the
kind of "spontaneous overflow of powerful feelings" that
Orpingalik so beautifully defines in his statement at the begin-
ning of this book. Through a combination of method, imagina-
tion and perseverance, a confluence of inspiration and tech-
nique, the song eventually achieved the shape which made it
suitable for performance.

Lastly, the internal evidence of the songs themselves very
clearly demonstrates an awareness of the craftsmanship that went
into composition. I have drawn an analogy between hunting
and composing skills. But certain recurring phrases and images
suggest an even closer connection between the songs and yet
another set of techniques. Jenness's comments on the incoher-
ence of many of the songs he collected is, in a sense, quite accur-
ate—for the European reader of his versions. But it begs the

question of whether the Eskimos were aware of this, and wanted it any other way. As Heq told Rasmussen, there are some songs that "ordinary people do not have to understand. The wisdom in them is often concealed . . ." (see note p. 117). Whether the song can be reduced to a prose meaning or not, it will always have emerged from a process in which the poet is searching, above all, for structure. The phrase "putting words together" that so frequently recurs, not only implies structure in itself, but it suggests that the manipulation of words is strongly associated with the exercise of power over concrete objects: objects and materials which are very often associated with the crafts:

> I, aya, am arranging
> I am trying to put together song this one,
> taking it apart, I aya
> why I wonder is it always on the tip of my tongue!
>> (Nakasuk, *Report of the Fifth Thule Expedition,*
>> Vol. 7. Not included in this book.)

> never heaping evil words
> on men . . .
>> (Umanatsiaq, *World*)

> My tongue can only put together words
> to make a little song.
> A mouth, a little mouth,
> can that be dangerous?
>> (Netsit, *Men's Impotence*)

> A bit of song comes back.
> I draw it to me like a friend.
>> (Uvlunuaq, *Song of a Mother*)

> I put some words together,
> I made a little song,
> I took it home one evening,
> mysteriously wrapped, disguised . . .
>> (Angmagssalik, *Song to a Miser*)

I weave together
bits of song to answer you . . .
(Piuvkaq, *The Wide Road of
Song*)

Let me cleave words,
sharp little words.
like the fire-wood
that I split with my axe.
(Kilimé, *The Abduction*)

The analogy with the crafts is implicit in the language. Words
(like snow, or bones, or reindeer skin) are part of the material
environment, and they have the sort of concrete property which
can be woven, wrapped up, carved and put together, for either
functional or aesthetic purposes. The Eskimos' perception of
the power and malleability of words would seem to provide
something of a clue as to how they raised their poetry to a level
beyond that of local interest. The interaction between the singer,
the experience and the language is externalised and made real in
the activity of composition; the words are carved at a distance
from the self, thus preserving what the self would otherwise
lose. That the Eskimo poet knew he was doing this was a con-
dition of his doing it well. I hope that the translations in this
collection will do justice to my belief that this is so.

T.L.

Eskimo Song Orpingalik

Songs are thoughts which are sung out with the breath when people let themselves be moved by a great force, and ordinary speech no longer suffices.

A person is moved like an ice-floe which drifts with the current. His thoughts are driven by a flowing force when he feels joy, when he feels fear, when he feels sorrow. Thoughts can surge in on him, causing him to gasp for breath, and making his heart beat faster. Something like a softening of the weather will keep him thawed. And then it will happen that we, who always think of ourselves as small, will feel even smaller. And we will hesitate before using words. But it will happen that the words that we need will come of themselves—

When the words that we need shoot up of themselves—we have a new song.

ORPINGALIK, Netsilik Eskimo Man

I: SONGS OF MOOD

NETSIT
(Copper Eskimo man, Musk Ox Folk)

Spirit Song

Do you hear
The voice from the deep!
  ajai-jija.
The voice from the deep!
  Ajai-jija.

I will visit
unclean women,
probe behind man,
break taboo.
Aj, let the lace of the boot hang loose.
  Ajai-jija.

Do you hear
the voice from the deep?
  Ajai-jija.
The voice from the deep!
  Ajai-jija.

I will visit
unclean women,
probe behind man,
break taboo.
Aj, smooth the wrinkles
from the rounded cheeks!
  Ajai-jija.
I walked out on the sea.
Marvelling, I heard
the voice from the deep,

the song of the sea.
I went out slowly,
pondering myself.
The vast young ice-floes sighed,
   ajai-jija
   ajai-jija.
Helping spirit seeks the feasting-house.

Song about the Reindeer, Musk Oxen, Women, and Men who want to Show Off

It's wonderful to see
the reindeer come down
from the forest,
and start pouring north
over the white tundra,
anxiously avoiding pit-falls in the snow.
    Jai-ja-jija.

And it's wonderful to see
the short-haired reindeer
in the early summer
start wandering.
    Jajai-ja-jija.

It's wonderful to see them
trotting back and forth
over the headlands,
searching for a crossing-place.
    Jai-ja-jija.

It's wonderful to see
the great musk-oxen
bunching up in herds
to guard themselves
against the dogs.
    Jajai-ja-jija.

It's wonderful to see
girls coming out
and visiting,
the men showing off,
the girls all telling little lies.
    Jai-ja-jija.

It's wonderful to see
the reindeer with their winter fur
returning to the woods,
anxiously avoiding us, the little men,
and following the ebb-mark of the sea,
with a rustle
and a creak of hoofs.
Oh, it's wonderful!
  Jajai-ja-jija.

Maybe—yes
it doesn't matter.
Maybe—yes.
I'll just sing about a man,
"The One at Boiling-Point",
who sat tight-lipped and frightened
among women.

Maybe—yes
it doesn't matter.
Maybe—yes.
I'll just sing about a man,
"The Reindeer-Belly",
who sat tight-lipped and frightened
among women.
His eyes augured ill,
curved like a horn
to carve into an eeling-fork.

Maybe—yes
it doesn't matter.
Maybe—yes.
I'll just sing about a man,
"The Axe",
who sat tight-lipped and frightened,
far, far away from people,
in solitude.

Maybe—yes
it doesn't matter.
Maybe—yes.
My tongue can only put together words
to make a little song.
A mouth, a little mouth,
can that be dangerous?

A little mouth,
that curves down at the corners
like a stick,
bent to form a kayak's rib.

I Wonder Where?

Deep down, deep down inside,
you can get cold with fear.
Deep down, deep down inside,
you can get cold with fear
because you married
one who stayed a child,
who never grew.
Yet no-one wanted to be like
"The Lightly Downed",
who grew up like
an average human being,
restless and unbalanced.

Deep down, deep down inside,
you can get cold with fear.
Deep down, deep down inside,
you can get cold with fear
because game flees from you.
I wonder where?
I wonder where?
The musk oxen,
and the great inland bear,
the reindeer-herds,
all take to flight.
I wonder where?

Dead Man's Song

(Dreamt by a man still living at the time of composition.)

I'm filled with joy
when the day dawns quietly
over the roof of the sky,
    aji, jai ja.

I'm filled with joy
when the sun rises slowly
over the roof of the sky,
    aji, jai ja.

But other times, I choke with fear:
a greedy swarm of maggots
eats into the hollows
of my collar-bone and eyes,
    aji, jai ja.

I lie here dreaming
how I choked with fear
when they shut me
in an ice-hut on the lake,
    aji, jai ja.

And I could not see
my soul would ever free itself
and get up to the hunting-grounds
of the sky,
    aji, jai ja.

Fear grew, and grew.
Fear overwhelmed me
when the fresh-water ice
snapped in the cold,
and the booming crack of the frost
grew into the sky,
    aji, jai ja.

Life was wonderful
in winter.
But did winter make me happy?
No, I always worried
about hides for boot-soles
and for boots:
and if there'd be enough
for all of us.
Yes, I worried constantly,
   aji, jai ja.

Life was wonderful
in summer.
But did summer make me happy?
No, I always worried
about reindeer skins and rugs for the
                        platform.
Yes, I worried constantly,
   aji, jai ja.

Life was wonderful
when you stood at your fishing-hole
on the ice.
But was I happy waiting at my fishing
                        hole?
No, I always worried
for my little hook,
in case it never got a bite.
Yes, I worried constantly,
   aji, jai ja.

Life was wonderful
when you danced in the feasting-house.
But did this make me any happier?
No, I always worried
I'd forget my song.
Yes, I worried constantly,
   aji, jai ja.

Life was wonderful . . .
And I still feel joy
each time the day-break
whitens the dark sky,
each time the sun
climbs over the roof of the sky,
   aji, jai ja.

TATILGAK
(Copper Eskimo man, Musk Ox Folk, Bathurst Inlet)

The Sun and the Moon and the Fear
of Loneliness

It's a fearful thing
to turn one's mind away,
and long for solitude
among a happy crowd of people.
    Ijaija-ja-ja.

It's a happy thing
to feel warmth
come to the great world,
and see the sun
follow its old footsteps
in the summer night.
    Ijaija-ja-ja.

It's a fearful thing
to feel the cold
return to the great world,
and see the moon—
now new, now full—
follow its old footsteps
in the winter night.
    Ijaija-ja-ja.

Where does all this go, I wonder?
For myself, I long to travel east!
But I'll never see
my father's brother,
whom my mind so longs
to open itself to.

A Forgotten Man's Song about the Winds

(Nobody knows who the composer of this song was, but his words are remembered.)

I wonder what the dear south wind
has on its mind
as it blows past?
Does it think about the small people
who live north of us?
Does it think of them,
as it blows past?

I wonder what the dear east wind
has on its mind
as it blows past?
Does it think of the small people
who live west of us?
Does it think of them,
as it blows past?

I wonder what the dear north wind
has on its mind
as it blows past?
Does it think of the small people
who live south of us?
Does it think of them,
as it blows past?

I wonder what the dear west wind
has on its mind
as it blows past?
Does it think of the small people
who live east of us?
Does it think of them,
as it blows past?

And what is on my mind
as I roam the land?

I think of all the living things
that can be seen :
the musk oxen that crowd together
in clusters on the tundra,
and the reindeer
lifting their antlers
above the mountain-tops !
It's precious game
I think of as I wander.

Bird Song

The great gull hovers
on wings spread wide
above us, above us.
He stares, I shout!
His head is white,
his beak gapes,
his small round eyes
look far, look sharp!
  Qutiuk! Qutiuk!

The great skua hovers
on wings spread wide
above us, above us.
He stares, I shout!
His head is black,
his beak gapes,
his small round eyes
look far, look sharp!
  Ijoq! Ijoq!

The great raven hovers
on wings spread wide
above us, above us.
He stares, I shout!
His head is blue-black,
his beak is sharp
(does it have teeth?)
His eyes squint!
  Qara! Qara!

And then there is the owl,
the great owl!
He hovers
on wings spread wide
above us, above us.

He stares, I shout!
His head is swollen,
his beak is hooked,
and his round eyes
have lids turned inside out,
red and heavy!
　Oroq! Oroq!

Isn't it delightful,
little river cutting through the gorge,
when you slowly approach it,
and trout hang behind stones
in the stream?
 Jajai-ija.

Isn't it delightful,
that *grassy* river bank?
Yet Willow Twig,
whom I so long to see again,
is lost to me.
So be it.
The winding of the river
through the gorge is lovely enough.
 Jajai-ija.

Isn't it delightful,
that bluish island of rocks out there,
as you slowly approach it?
So what does it matter
that the blowing spirit of the air
wanders over the rocks:
the island is so beautiful,
when, driving steadily,
you gain on it.

QERNERTOQ
(Copper Eskimo woman, Musk Ox Folk)

The Widow's Song

Why will people
have no mercy on me?
Sleep comes hard
since Maula's killer
showed no mercy.
Ijaja-ijaja.

Was the agony I felt so strange,
when I saw the man I loved
thrown on the earth
with bowed head?
Murdered by enemies,
worms have for ever
deprived him
of his homecoming.
Ijaja-ijaja.

He was not alone
in leaving me.
My little son
has vanished
to the shadow-land.
Ijaja-ijaja.

Now I'm like a beast
caught in the snare
of my hut.
Ijaja-ijaja.

Long will be my journey
on the earth.
It seems as if
I'll never get beyond
the foot-prints that I make. . . .

A worthless amulet
is all my property :
while the northern light
dances its sparkling steps
in the sky.

HEQ
(Copper Eskimo man, Musk Ox Folk)

Sick Man's Song

Soul, where have you hidden?
Let me fetch you!
Have you travelled to the south of those
who live south of us?
Let me fetch you!

Soul, where have you hidden?
Let me fetch you!
Have you travelled to the east of those
who live east of us?
Let me fetch you!

Soul, where have you hidden?
Let me fetch you!
Have you travelled to the north of those
who live north of us?
Let me fetch you!

Soul, where have you hidden?
Let me fetch you!
Have you travelled to the west of those
who live west of us?
Let me fetch you!

Soul, where have you hidden?
Have you travelled past us, altogether?
Travelled past the people
who live far from us?
Let me fetch you!

QERRAQ
(Copper Eskimo man, Musk Ox Folk)

Song of a Diffident Man

I am one who always
has the stream against him.
Slowly, slowly I press on.
If I went to visit
people who live south of us,
it was always difficult.
But eventually I reached
the lonely people
living at the far end of the fjord.

I am one who always
has the stream against him.
Slowly, slowly I press on.
If I wanted to hunt reindeer
near the "Little Spring"
it was always difficult.
At length I did surprise
the black musk oxen
that bellowed on the river-bank.

It was always hard
to join the men up front
who caught the seals :
yet I always kept
my harpoon ready.
 Jaijaija.

It was always hard
to join the men up front
who killed the reindeer :

yet I always carried
arrows on my back.
   Jaijaija.

It was always hard
to join the happy company
that sang in the feasting-house :
for I never could remember
the words of my little song
in the drum-dance.
I was always holding back.
I was such a humble creature.
Everything was difficult.

KINGMERUT
(Copper Eskimo man, Ellis River, Queen Maud's Sea)

Hunger

Fear hung over me.
I dared not try
to hold out in my hut.

Hungry and chilled,
I stumbled inland,
tripping, falling constantly.

At Little Musk Ox Lake
the trout made fun of me;
they wouldn't bite.

On I crawled,
and reached the Young Man's River
where I caught salmon once.

I prayed
for fish or reindeer
swimming in the lake.

My thought
reeled into nothingness,
like run-out fishing-line.

Would I ever find firm ground?
I staggered on,
muttering spells as I went.

IVALUARDJUK
(Iglulik Eskimo man, Lyon Inlet)

A Hunting Memory

Cold and mosquitoes
are torments
that never come together.
I lie down on the ice,
I lie down on the ice and snow
so my jaws chatter.
This is I!
Aja-aja-ja.

Is it memories
of the seasons,
of the seasons,
(mosquitoes swarming)
of the seasons
(ice paralysing)
make the mind swoon,
as I stretch my limbs out
on the ice?
This is I!
Aja-aja-ja.

Aj! But songs
require strength,
and I search
for words. Yes, I!
Aja-aja-ja.

Aj! I raise my head and see
the subject of my song:
the broad-antlered reindeer!

25

Powerfully I hurled
the spear and throwing-pole,
my weapon tethering the bull
right in the middle of the loin
He trembled, and he fell.
And then lay still.

Aj! But songs
require strength,
and I search
for words.
Here is the song.
Here is the memory.
It's only I who sings.
Aja-aja-haja-haja!

UVAVNUK
(Iglulik Eskimo woman)

Moved

(A song that would always send the shaman Uvavnuk into a trance.)

> The great sea stirs me.
> The great sea sets me adrift,
> it sways me like the weed
> on a river-stone.
>
> The sky's height stirs me.
> The strong wind blows through my mind.
> It carries me with it,
> so I shake with joy.

ORULO
(Iglulik Eskimo woman)

Greeting to the Women of the Feasting-house

Important archery contests and ball-games were always concluded with wife-swapping, when the songs of the evening had been sung. To symbolise this festivity, the women arrived at the snow-hut carrying great gulls' feathers, held high above their heads. Here is the song with which they were received:

> Women, women,
> young women!
> Aj, they come,
> in fine new furs,
> women, women,
> young women!
>
> Aj, they carry festive gulls' wings
> in their fine white gloves.
> See, they sway,
> see, they call,
> and blush with eagerness!
>
> Women, women,
> young women!
> Aj-aj,
> aj-aj-aj!
>
> The edges of their long skirts
> ripple as they come.
> See how beautifully
> they glide towards the men,
> who joyfully await
> rewards of victory!
> Women, women,
> young women!

TUTLIK
(Iglulik Eskimo woman, Aivilik Folk, Lyon Inlet)

Dancing Song

Two little girls squat opposite each other, and hop up and down, singing
repeatedly. They sing again and again, hopping faster all the time.

Aj-ja-japa-pé.
Bring out your hair-ornaments!
We're only girls
rejoicing with each other!
Aj-ja-japapé.

Difficult times,
shortages of meat
have smitten everyone:
stomachs hollow,
meat-trays empty.
Aj-ja-japapé.

Can you see out there?
The men are coming home,
dragging seals
towards our village!
Aj-ja-japapé.

Joy has distorted
everything in sight:
the leather boats lift themselves
away from their ropes,
the straps follow them,
the earth itself
floats freely in the air!
Aj-ja-japapé.

Plenty visits us again:
times when feasts
bind us together.
Aj-ja-japapé.

Do you recognise
the smell of boiling pots,
and blubber squelching
in the corner of the bench?
Aj-ja-japapé, hu-hue!
Joyfully we welcome
those who bring us wealth!

ATQARALAQ
(Caribou Eskimo woman)

Two Beast Fables

1. *The Proposal of the Owl*

A little snow bunting sat on a hummock, and wept because her husband
had been slain by a hunter. A great fat owl came up and sang:

> Fool, to lament
> that wretched little husband
> with his spears of grass!
> I'll marry you myself!

The snow bunting replied:

> Get married to an owl?
> Not with those coarse feathers of yours,
> that clumsy beak,
> thick calves,
> domed forehead,
> no neck!

The enraged owl struck the little bunting on the breast. When she cried
out in pain, he only taunted her:

> That's woman for you:
> sharp-tongued enough,
> but poke her breast
> and she'll start whimpering!

With that they flew off in separate directions.

2. *Song of the Lemming*

On a cold winter's day, a little lemming came out of his warm hole. He looked
about him, shivered, shook himself, and sang:

> The sky,
> like a vast belly,
> arches itself
> around my burrow.
> The air is clear,
> no clouds in sight:
> icy weather! Aiee!
> I'm freezing! freezing!

AKJARTOQ
(Caribou Eskimo woman)

An Old Woman's Song

Alas, I draw breath heavily,
my lungs breathe heavily,
as I call for my song.

When the news arrived
of far-off friends,
starving for winter game,
I wanted to sing:
to invoke the words from above,
the music from above.
Hajaja!

I forget the fire in my chest,
and the wheeze of the lungs
while I sing,
and I remember the old times
when I was strong.

These were times
when no-one rivalled me
at flensing seal;
when all alone, I boned and cut
the lean flesh
of three great reindeer-bulls
for drying!

Look: delicious slices
spread out on the mountain-stones,
while the sun rides up the sky
in the cool morning,
in the cool morning!

KIBKARJUK
(Caribou Eskimo woman, Barren Grounds)

Work Song

I'm only a little woman,
who's happy to slave,
happy to toil.
Anxious to be useful,
I pluck willow-flowers
that remind me
of the great wolf's beard.

I wear holes in my kamiks
when I walk far out
to pluck the willow-flowers,
that bring to mind
the great wolf's beard,
the great wolf's beard.

Song of the Rejected Woman

(Kibkarjuk remembers when she was her husband's favourite wife, and was allowed to hunt caribou herself.)

Inland,
far inland go my thoughts,
my mournful thoughts.
To never leave the woman's bench
is too much to endure:
I want to wander inland,
far inland.
 Ija-je-ja.

My thoughts return
to hunting:
animals, delightful food!
To never leave the woman's bench
is too much to endure:
I want to wander inland,
far inland.
 Ija-je-ja.

I hunted like
the men:
I carried weapons,
shot a reindeer bull,
a reindeer cow and calf,
yes, slew them with my arrows,
with my arrows,
one evening towards winter,
as the sky-dusk fell
far inland.
 Ija-je-ja.

This is what I think about,
this is what I struggle with,
while inland, under falling snow,
the earth turns white,
far inland.
   Ija-je-ja.

ULIVFAK
(Caribou Eskimo man, Barren Grounds)

The Spring of Youth

Sadly I recall
the early spring of my youth :
the snow melted,
the ice broke,
long before usual.

I stood scenting game
in the hot sun,
muscles taut,
sweat dripping from my face.

Look! Someone's out there
on the slapping lake-water,
slowly dragging reindeer
behind a kayak,
or noisily taking leave
for a dangerous sea-journey.
Could that be me?

As a hunter on land
I was undistinguished.
My arrows seldom reached
the reindeer in the hills.
But from a kayak,
hunting in the wake
of swimming bulls,
I had no match.

Thus I still re-live
the early spring of youth.
Old men seek strength
in the thaw of younger days.

37

ORPINGALIK
(Netsilik Eskimo man)

My Breath

This is what I call my song, because it is as important for me to sing it, as it is to draw breath.

This is my song: a powerful song.
Unaija-unaija.
Since autumn I have lain here,
helpless and ill,
as if I were my own child.

Sorrowfully, I wish my woman
to another hut,
another man for refuge,
firm and safe as the winter-ice.
Unaija-unaija.

And I wish my woman
a more fortunate protector,
now I lack the strength
to raise myself from bed.
Unaija-unaija.

Do you know yourself?
How little of yourself you understand!
Stretched out feebly on my bench,
my only strength is in my memories.
Unaija-unaija.

Game! Big game,
chasing ahead of me!
Allow me to re-live that!
Let me forget my frailty,
by calling up the past!
Unaija-unaija.

I bring to mind that great white one,
the polar bear,
approaching with raised hind-quarters,
his nose in the snow—
convinced, as he rushed at me,
that of the two of us,
he was the only male!
Unaija-unaija.
Again and again he threw me down :
but spent at last,
he settled by a hump of ice,
and rested there,
ignorant that I was going to finish him.
He thought he was the only male around!
But I too was a man!
Unaija-unaija.

Nor will I forget that great blubbery one,
the fjord-seal, that I slaughtered
from an ice-floe before dawn,
while friends at home
were laid out like the dead,
feeble with hunger,
famished with bad luck.
I hurried home,
laden with meat and blubber,
as though I were just running across the ice
to view a breathing-hole.
Yet this had been an old and cunning bull,
who'd scented me at once—
but before he had drawn breath,
my spear was sinking
through his neck.

This is how it was.
Now I lie on my bench,
too sick to even fetch
a little seal oil for my woman's lamp.

Time, time scarcely seems to pass,
though dawn follows dawn,
and spring approaches the village.
Unaija-unaija.

How much longer must I lie here?
How long? How long must she go begging
oil for the lamp,
reindeer-skins for her clothes,
and meat for her meal?
I, a feeble wretch :
she, a defenceless woman.
Unaija-unaija.

Do you know yourself?
How little of yourself you understand!
Dawn follows dawn,
and spring is approaching the village.
   Unaija-unaija.

UVLUNUAQ
(Netsilik Eskimo woman, Pelly Bay)

Song of a Mother

A young man had killed his hunting companion in a fit of rage. The murderer's
mother sang this song to express her grief:

Ejaja-eja.
A bit of song comes back.
I draw it to me like a friend.
    Ejaja-eja.

I ought, I suppose, to be ashamed
of the child I once carried on my back,
when I heard he'd left the settlement.
They're right to tell me so:
I ought to be ashamed.
    Ejaja-eja.

I am ashamed:
because he didn't have a mother
who was faultless
as the clear sky,
wise and without folly.
Now that he's the butt
of everybody's tongue,
this evil talk will finish him.
    Ejaja-eja.

He has become the burden
of my age.
But far from being
properly ashamed,
I'm envious of others
when they break up

after feasts, and set off
with crowds of friends
behind them, waving on the ice.
   Ejaja-eja.

I remember one mild spring.
We'd camped near Cross-Eye Lake.
Our footsteps sank
with a soft creak
into half-thawed snow.
I stayed near the men,
like a tame animal.
But when the news
about the murder came,
and that he'd fled,
the ground heaved under me
like a mountain,
and I stood on its summit,
and I staggered.

IKINILIK
(Utkuhikjalik man)

Upstream

Song of an old man trout-fishing from the ice.

I often go back
to my little song,
and hum it patiently
at my fishing-hole on the ice.
Again and again,
I hum that simple little song.
I, who all too soon
get weary when I fish,
watchfully angling,
trying to tempt
the blue-black salmon with their glossy scales,
who swim,
    upstream.

Blowingly cold, my vigil on the ice.
I soon give up.
When I get home with insufficient catch
I say it was the fish that failed,
    upstream.

Yet it's wonderful to roam
the snow-soft river-ice,
as long as I support myself,
    upstream.

But now my life has slid
far from the height of the mountain-tops,
deep into the valley of old age,
    upstream.

If I hunt on land,
or try to fish,
it isn't long
before I'm sinking to my knees,
stricken with weariness,
    upstream.

I'll never feel
the surge of strength I used to get,
when I hunt inland
for my hut and those I feed,
    upstream.

I'm just a worn-out hunter now,
who'll never breathe
the great winds of the hunting-grounds again.

Yet my body's still alive
and my stomach still craves
feasts of meat.

My manhood is reduced :
an unblest fisherman,
who makes his hole
in sea or river ice,
where no trout bite,
    upstream.

Yet life is full
of interest and excitement !
I only . . .
I only have my song,
though it too glides away from me,
    upstream.

For I'm just an ordinary hunter
who never inherited singing
from the bird-song of the sky.

PIUVKAQ
(Utkuhikjalik man, Great Fish River)

Delight in Singing

It's wonderful
to make up songs :
but all too many of them fail.

It's wonderful
to have your wishes granted :
but all too often
they slip by.

It's wonderful
to hunt reindeer :
but all too seldom
you succeed,
standing like a bright fire
on the plain.

EAST GREENLAND
(From Angmagssalik)

Song to a Miser

A man was once discovered to have been in the habit of fetching meat from his store during the night while other people in the house were asleep. He ate his fill without letting his companions share the enjoyment. As soon as he had finished, he wrapped the remnants in a skin and hid them under the bed. One of his mates later took revenge by composing the following song which he recited one evening to the malicious delight of the audience. It is said that the miser was so ashamed that he never indulged in secret eating again:

I put some words together,
I made a little song,
I took it home one evening,
mysteriously wrapped, disguised.
Underneath my bed it went:
nobody was going to share it,
nobody was going to taste it!
I wanted it for me! me! me!
Secret, undivided!

Song to Spring

Winter has been long and hard, and the people of the village have suffered privation. Everyone is exhausted, and many believe that they're not going to live until spring. Then a man goes out along the coast in a kayak, where the first open water is beginning to appear. He comes to a hillside, which he climbs so as to have a view of any openings in the ice where he can hunt seal. Weak, and faint with hunger, he labours up the hill, until he discovers a snowdrift which the warmth of the sun is loosening from the mountain. He feels such happiness that he bursts out in song:

Aja-ha   aja-ha
I was out in my kayak
making towards land.
Aja-ha   aja-ha
I came to a snow-drift
that had just begun to melt.
Aja-hai-ja   aja-hai-ja
And I knew that it was spring:
we'd lived through winter!
Aja-hai-ja   aja-hai-ja
And I was frightened
I would be too weak,
too weak
to take in all that beauty!
Aja-hai-ja
Aja-hai-ja
Aja-ha.

Song to the Sea

All winter, the sea on the East coast of Greenland lies frozen and inaccessible to sledge-riders. But when spring approaches, and the ice starts loosening, good days for daring hunters have arrived.

I'm not an empty, stubborn man,
bored and taciturn,
Ava-ajaja, ajaja-aja.
I climbed the hills of Sermilik,
and gazed out at the sea,
the great sea,
ava-ajaja, ajaja-aja.

Vast ice-floes
lay scattered along the coast;
a glacier carved its way
into the deep,
and the Uigordlit rocks
stood like pillars
above the waters,
ava-ajaja-aja.

I grew dizzy,
my breath laboured,
and it seemed to me
my life was destined to be short,
too short,
ava-ajaja, ajaja-aja.

Song about Narwhales

In his youth, a great hunter once lived on a fjord which is famous for its plentiful herds of narwhales. An old man now, he returns to the village of his youth, and once more sees the narwhales playing in the sea. He senses the feebleness that age has brought on him; he feels faint with grief, and he seizes his drum and sings:

Ijâja-â-ijajâ, ajê,
let me try to turn these thoughts,
these heavy thoughts,
away, away,
ijâja-â-ijajâ-ajê.

Let me try to swallow grief,
like swallowing a sob,
ijâja-â-ijajâ-ajê.

Let words of song bear sorrow off,
let singing words breathe sorrow from my throat.

Let my clumsy little song
lift sorrow from my mind,
ijâja-â-ijajâ-ajê.

Impossible, alas,
to tear pain from the throat.
Impossible
to give way at the bursting point, to tears,
ijâja-â-ijajâ-ajê.

My eyes are tired,
my eyes are worn,
my eyes will never watch again
a run of narwhales
as they shoot up from the depths,
and break against the waves.
Never will my muscles tremble,
gripping the harpoon again,
ijâja-â-ijajâ-ajê.

Now I only wish
the souls of all the sea-beasts that I killed
might help me lift these heavy thoughts :
and the memory of great hunts
lift me out of weak old age!
Ijâja-â-ijajâ-ajê.

So let me breathe a song
about the game I hunted,
and sing about my narwhales :
the narwhale herds
that broke the foam
close to my village,
ijâja-â-ijajâ-ajê.

Sometimes their throaty call
would come in moans,
sometimes in shrill whinnyings
as they blew,
and families of them gathered
on the surface, resting.
This is what I sing about,
this is what reminds me of my youth.
And my song bursts from my throat
with my breath.

WEST GREENLAND
(Umanatsiaq)

Ptarmigan

On the top of a snowdrift
in the tundra,
stood a little ptarmigan.
Its eyelids were red,
its back was brown,
and right between its buttocks
sat the sweetest little arse.

(Umanatsiaq)

Words

Amaija-ai, ja-jai, ai-ja,
I'm a timid man—
a quietly-spoken one—
never mocking,
never heaping evil words
on men.
That's my way,
that's how I am,
amaja-ja.
Words cause movement,
words bring calm,
words tell the truth,
and words tell lies,
amaja-ja-ja!

(Umanatsiaq)

Love-Making

Ajaija-ja,
my playmate
ja-ja-jai-ja,
fingers me
between the legs,
hajaijaja,
she gives her body
haijaijaja-jaija—
and tears the leather bracelets
from my wrists.

(Southern Upernivik)

A Little Song

I sing a little song,
someone else's worn little song,
but I sing it as if it were my own,
my own dear little song.
In this way, I play
with a secondhand song,
and give it life again.

II: HUNTING SONGS

IGPAKUHAK
(Copper Eskimo man, Victoria Land)

Hymn to the Spirit of the Air

A religious song to be performed wearing a head-decoration made from the
skin of the sacred Great Northern Diver.

I stand here humbly
with extended arms,
for the spirit of the air
has brought down game for me!

I stand here
surrounded by great joy,
for a reindeer with tall antlers
carelessly exposed his flanks to me!

Ah, how I crouched
in my hunter's hide!
But scarcely had I
glimpsed his flanks,
than my arrow pierced them.
haunch to haunch.

And then, beloved reindeer,
as you pissed there,
as you fell,
I was surrounded by great joy!

I stand here humbly
with extended arms,
for the spirit of the air
has brought down game for me!

I stand here humbly
with extended arms,
surrounded by great joy:
an old seal-bull
was blowing through his breathing-hole,
and I, a little man,
stood upright over him.
The tension
made my body longer,
till I drove my harpoon down,
and tied him
to the harpoon-rope.

AUA
(Iglulik Eskimo man, Lyon Inlet)

Reindeer

I wriggled silently through the swamp,
carrying bow and arrow in my mouth.
The marsh was broad, the water icy cold,
and there was no cover in sight.

Slowly, soaked, invisible,
I crawled within range.
The reindeer were eating;
they grazed the juicy moss
without concern,
till my arrow sank
tremblingly deep
into the bull's side.

Terrified, the unsuspecting herd
hastily scattered,
and vanished at the sharpest trot
to shielding hills.

Polar Bear

I saw a polar bear
on an ice-drift.
He seemed harmless as a dog,
who comes running towards you,
wagging his tail.
But so much
did he want to get at me
that when I jumped aside
he went spinning on the ice.
We played this game of tag
from morning until dusk.
But then, at last, I tired him out,
and ran my spear into his side.

Walrus

The sea lay shining brightly
near my hut.
I couldn't sleep.

I paddled out.
A walrus came up
by the boat.

He was too close
for a harpoon-throw.
So I drove it
down and into him,
and the float went hopping
across the water.

But up he came,
and laid his flippers
just like elbows
on the surface,
as he tried to tear
the float to bits.

He tired himself in vain:
an unborn lemming's skin
(protective amulet)
was sewn to it.
Blowing angrily,
he gathered all his strength,
but I closed in
and put him out of pain.

So listen, boastful men
from distant fjords,
so eager always to draw breath

in praise of your own skill :
fill your lungs
with songs
about the daring exploits of a stranger!

IGJUGARJUK
(Caribou Eskimo man, Barren Grounds)

Musk Oxen

Jai-jai-jai,
ja-ajai-jai!
I ran as fast as possible,
and reached them on the plain :
the great musk oxen,
with black, glossy hair.
Hajai-ja-haja!

It was the first view I had had of them,
grazing the flowers,
feeding on the plain,
far from the mountain where I stood;
and in my ignorance,
I thought how small they were!
But they rose out of the earth,
as I drew within range :
vast, black animals,
far from the village,
in distant areas
where happy hunting's done.

AVANÉ
(Caribou Eskimo man, Barren Grounds)

On the Look Out

Impatient and excited,
I watch for reindeer in the hills.
Do I hunt in vain
because I'm old and slower than I was?
I, who once shot arrows
standing upright,
without having to take aim,
and a broad-antlered
reindeer-bull
would tumble down the hillside
with its muzzle deep in the clay.

III: SONGS OF DERISION

IGPAKUHAK
(Copper Eskimo man, Victoria Land)

Longing for Song-Contest

They say it is a joy
to listen to the song,
a joy to listen
when a famous singer lifts his voice,
and rocks in dance.
And look:
when the famous singer lifts his voice,
and dances to the drum,
then all the ermine-skins
that decorate his fur-coat flutter!

It rings and buzzes in my ears!
And it's all their fault,
the people-down-there-
by-the-little-trout-stream's fault!
I long for contests in the feasting-house,
the little feasting-house of Bony One:
the one I always challenge to a sing.
and yet I don't forget
how thoroughly one pities
the victim of the fight,
made lonely by the song of mockery,
immediately the contest finishes.

My ears! my ears!
It rings and buzzes in my ears!
I long for contests in the feasting-house!
And it's all their fault,
the people-down-there-
by-the-little-trout-stream's fault!

PIUVKAQ
(Utkuhikjalik man)

The Wide Road of Song

The hunter Qaqortingneq had been out of his mind with fury because his uncle, Piuvkaq, had eaten up one of his largest caches of musk ox meat, during a spell of unsuccessful winter hunting. He was so enraged, that he threatened his uncle's life. As a result of this, Piuvkaq sang this song of derision:

Eager to breathe out,
I have prepared
this little bit of song,
along the wide road of the song:
mocking in expression,
well composed,
pointed in words,
out west, out west!

Here I am,
yes, fresh awake,
and ready for defence!

It was a winter night in the dark season.
While others lay asleep,
a sound approached:
it hit my ear,
it hit my ear,
out west, out west!

It said my kinsman,
nick-named Tight Belt,
started raving,
made a frenzied scene,
on the firm winter ice.

Petty and ill-tempered,
he gabbled about stolen food,
when everybody else was starving.

Here I am,
yes, fresh awake,
and ready for defence!

In a bitter spell
of hopeless winter hunting,
we tried to save our lives
with a little meat from your store.
That was all!

Should hunters
be so miserly?
Out west, out west!
But out you came,
with a knife in your hand,
meat-mad, raging!

In my innocence,
I didn't understand
what you were shouting.
Murder never crossed my mind!
Foolishly, I quite forgot
that—aj—a miser's mind
could be obscured like that!

But here I am
to douse you with my mockery,
to deluge you with laughter:
a cheap correction,
easy punishment!

I weave together
bits of song to answer you.
The voice must ring out clear
to drown that voice of yours!
I'm strong enough :
just feeble at inventing wickedness.
Fist-fighting's more my style
than shouted tongue-disputes.
Words all too often disappear :
words disappear like hills in mist.

KANGITSUKAQ AND KUITSE
(Angmagssalik, East Greenland)

Song of Derision about Wife-Swapping

Kangitsukaq (The Little Headless One) once challenged Kuitse (The Spilt Water) before the latter was quite grown up. Kuitse did not forget the challenge, and reported himself ready for song-contest the moment he was a grown man.

A gust of air hangs over me!
I'm like this,
I can't help it,
Sing I must,
and open up my mouth
to words and notes.
Perhaps it may turn out a useful song,
a song that finds its mark
in somebody who needs it :
useful to some easily-disgusted man,
a man who breaks a friendship suddenly,
a man who's soon disgusted with the friend
he swaps his wife with!

You are such a man, my enemy!
Isn't it true
you quickly broke with Angutange,
with whom you'd shared
the pleasant game
of putting out the lamps with women?

Isn't it true
you soon got bored and sick of him—
and since then, been a lonely man,
with no one to swap wives with you?

But look at me!
Good men flock around me
and present their women
in exchange for mine.
They come in trust
because they know
I'm not a reckless man,
rejecting women,
separating man from wife.

This is how I am:
I won't get hurt,
I won't risk witchcraft
and revenge.
I love women.
I'm a woman-lover.
I don't let them pass me by.

Evil news was often
brought us from Cape Dan,
when men in kayaks came and visited.
It was pleasant things one heard!
It has been said
(Yes, a little rumour reached my ear)
that my opponent
nearly killed his wife-swap friend!

The reason?
They say it was a dog
he had presented to his friend,
a token from the days
they'd happily swapped wives.
But later, he forgot those joys,
and tried to kill his gift,
to kill the dog.

Yes, this is what he's like,
my contest-enemy.
And as I sing
amusing little details
come to mind :

I was out at sea, on winter ice,
travelling by sleigh outside the village,
hunting bear.
I saw a mother with her cub,
come wandering,
the young one in the mother's tracks.
I caught up with them,
and while my barking dogs
forced them to stop,
I quietly
sought the adult out.

His dogs never would approach
that sort of game :
that wretched team
is hardly trained to hunt.
They'll never even see
a living bear :
pitiful bags of skin and bones they are,
with coats which could at most
be used for covering a kayak.
Yes, this how my song of mockery's turned out.
I hope it reaches folk
who want a bit of entertainment !

Kuitse answers :

Look at him !
Just look at what he's like, my song-adversary !
Listen to his rant,
and how he uses that great mouth,
like everybody in his village !

He finds nothing difficult,
nothing's difficult to call to mind.
But I'm more careful in my choice of words,
and wouldn't dare to sing of everything that passed.

Now, there were my male cousins,
and all my dearest female cousins,
who sailed off on a long journey,
and never returned.
All my loved ones
this man mocked in song,
this thin-shitter, this fat-belly!

So what remains for me to sing about,
now you've roared your head off
about things I'd rather not recall?
You always were so amiable,
always had such gentle ways:
you haven't got an evil reputation to expose.
And yet . . . what was it I heard . . .
What was the rumour
that *did* reach my ears?

IT WAS YOU WHO TRIED TO KILL MIGSSUARNIANGA,
THE MAN WITH CRIPPLED LEGS!

When I heard the talk,
I had to stop and ask myself:
could such a carcase-eater,
fat of belly, round of loins,
have strength in him to kill?
Well, it was cunning of you
to pick a paralytic,
being such a lazy-bones,
whom no one equals dozing
on the hot fur-covers of the bench!

74

KILIME AND EQERQO
(*Angmagssalik, East Greenland*)

The Abduction

Kilime sings:

Let me cleave words,
sharp little words,
like the fire-wood
that I split with my axe!
A song of old times,
a gust of soul from ancestors,
a song of oblivion for my wife,
a song to soothe the longing
overwhelming me!
This loud-mouth's
ravished her, belittled her:
a wretched cannibal
who loves to eat men's flesh,
in times of scarcity!

Eqerqo replies:

Shameless impudence!
Half-hearted coward!
You want to put the blame on me
and scare me, with your mockery?
But I'm indifferent
to the risk of being killed.
Look: it's *my* wife that you sing about.
She was yours once,
but you weren't quite so loving
at the time.

When she was all alone,
you never praised her
in your fighting challenge-songs.
Now she's mine,
and won't go visiting
false lovers, womanisers,
singing beautifully
in strange tents.

AGDLIARTORTOQ*
AND MIGSSUARNIANGA†
(Angmagssalik, East Greenland)

Contempt

Agdliartortoq sings:

I never worried
when I hunted in my kayak
out at sea,
far out at sea.
But late one evening,
as I reached the village,
having caught no seals,
a thought slid through my mind,
and I muttered softly to myself:
"Mysterious great ocean,
which shaman is to
fill you with fat seals,
fill you with fat seals?
Which shaman, game-provider?

If only I were parentless—
an orphan, who's despised by men,
who's forced to turn to spirits,
and with age, become adept
in hidden sorceries—
I'd be capable of filling up
the depths with seals myself!

But of course I'm just
an average sort of hunter,
with no magic powers,
without a shaman's cunning!"

* "The Constantly Growing One"   † "The Sucker"

77

All these these things I muttered in my modesty,
when a wonderful idea
shone through my worrying:
Let the generous little Sucker
fill the sea with seals,
and bring the village
joys of game, the joys of game!

They came to mind, these thoughts,
they came to mind
in pure exuberance, in jest,
because I knew
that he was everybody's fool,
that he was everybody's fool!

Wasn't it the Sucker's divinations,
clumsy lies,
that made us all believe
his wretched mongrel
came from the moon-spirit of the sky,
sent to punish breach of taboo,
to punish breach of sacred taboo?

That lie wreaked havoc.
Alas, his own aunt
almost froze to death
because the family, in its terror,
hid the old woman in a kayak
when they fled
into the fierce night-cold,
the clever shaman in the lead,
the clever shaman in the lead!
Aj, prodigious humbug,
who believes his lies,
believes his lies!

And then, of course, we know too well
the savage sleigh-dog of the moon,
the angry passage watch-dog of the moon,
glossy in its fur and colouring!
Aj, a shit-heap mongrel!

Aj-aj-aj, all this drowns
in the wild laughter of the village!
Incomparable shaman,
who believes his lies,
and runs from his own dog!

Migssuarnianga answers:

What shall I do?
What shall I do today?
I'm scarcely short of words,
so let me sing!

I was out at sea in a kayak,
north of the Great Sound,
gazing often to the south.
I was longing, longing
for a man whom I could hold
an honest singing-contest with.

At last I had my way:
took him to the village,
and gave him a thundering song of mockery!
Aj, aj, the thrust of my forehead closed his eye!
I was hard
with words and ringing whacks,
because he started on me
with a frightful mouth,
yes, a frightful mouth,
with evil poisonous abuse.
Aj, aj! a violent, ringing whack,
and a thrust of my forehead
closed his eye!

79

So think a little,
and don't bloat yourself with words!
Whom are you attacking?
Who is it you're shouting at,
with your short-winded rant?
You know nothing of
the people of the west,
the people of the sea,
the people of Cape Dan!
Keep your distance from them!
Keep your distance
from the masters
of the art of kayaking!
the people of the west,
the sons of the wave,
the people of Cape Dan!

AUTARUTA
(Igdluluarsuit man, East Greenland)

Challenge

The hunter Kunigssarfik ("The One with whom One Usually Rubs Noses")
had killed four of the Autarutas (The Wife-Boat) family with a spell.
Autaruta composed this challenge after the event, and sang it in the presence
of all the inhabitants of his village. Kunigssarfik never replied to his young
adversary, but fled in the wife-boat with his family. None of them returned,
but vanished without a trace among the ice-floes of the fjords.

Timidly, I search for words:
a young man
challenging a life-long enemy,
down there and south,
down there and south . . .

My enemy is great,
a mighty man,
down there and south,
down there and south . . .

My fate?
A short life, I suppose.
You, experienced in sorcery,
soul-thief, murderer,
and I a mere beginner,
a small and groping shaman.
Kill me then,
and steal my soul!
I have no family,
am lonely in the tribe,
down there and south,
down there and south . . .

Life, I suppose,
my fate, my days,
was all I cared about.
I therefore searched
for strength to live
through spirit-gifts:
a dog transformed
into a girl.
I took her,
she became my wife.
And you are impotent
to kill me with your curse,
down there and south,
down there and south . . .

Aj-aj, you always boasted noisily,
as though you were a man,
a proper man!
Don't push forward,
but leave quietly:
it's only big men
who puff their chests,
down there and south,
down there and south . . .

Ridiculous wizard!
What was it that I heard?
When "your highness"
calls on spirits,
you hide beneath the reindeer-skins,
behind your wife,
down there and south,
down there and south . . .

Rumour mocks:
aj, aj, aj,
gossip's busy
with The Mug, The Kisser,
the great shaman!
Is it true
that while you hid behind her, once,
your woman threw
a pail of icy water in your face?
Up you jumped,
bereft of wind and voice,
greeted by laughter,
drowned in shame,
Down there and south,
down there and south . . .

You're like a child
who whines and whimpers
all day long:
imploring everyone in vain
to give you husbands for your girls.
Hide! Disappear!
Find a lid
for your disgusting face!
See how your woman grieves
at all the shame you cause!
Down there and south,
down there and south . . .

My anger rises
as I mock you in my song,
unworthy villager.
You plotted evil,
committed murder and witchcraft,
murder and witchcraft,
ambushed and then slew my kin,
down there and south,
down there and south . . .

I had wonderful hunting,
up there and east,
up there and east :
the harpoon flew from my hand,
I slaughtered the fierce seal-bulls
with a single thrust,
up there and east,
up there and east . . .
With a single thrust,
I'll kill you too,
because you killed,
because you killed my family.

Once, rowing in a wild sea
by a reef,
where the waves were breaking,
I was seized with rage,
and flung my harpoon
at the cliff,
deep in the cliff.
The splashing of the water
calmed my mind,
up there and east,
up there and east . . .

Let us meet then,
youth and age :
one must die!
The song is evil;
one of us must die
from wounds.

PANINGUAQ
AND SAPANGAJAGADLEQ
(Southern Upernivik, West Greenland)

Dispute between Women

Songs of derision from a contest between Paninguaq (Little Daughter) and
her cousin Sapangajagadleq (The Pearl)

Little Daughter dances and sings:

It seems high time
I challenged you to song-contest!
Yes, my anger wakes!

I was out fetching fire
(domesticated as ever)
when you, in foolish vanity
began to flaunt yourself
before my step-father.
Do I lie or speak the truth?
Come forward: test me,
while my anger grows!

The Pearl jumps forward, dances and sings:

Come over to this side,
those who will defend me!
Take the wick of the lamp,
dip it in oil, light it,
allow the light
to fall on Little Daughter's face!
Do you hear me, cousin?
Do I lie or speak the truth?
I took you by surprise one day
in bed with Asarpana!

Mock her with me,
those who take my side!
Take her, friends,
and throw her to the ground!
Cousin, you don't still think
that you're a match for me?
Let's close our fists and punch!
Come, we'll have a race:
the winner takes the loser's man!

At this point, The Pearl jumps forward again, with a song intended to make
the audience laugh:

Ija-ja-hrra
ajai-jai-hrra,
aj-ja-a-ha!
Oh let me be
a little naughty!
Ai-ja-a-ha!
Just a little bad!
If only there were
someone who would stroke,
or only touch my cunt:
I shouldn't then
be angry or resent
another woman
smiling at my man!
Ai-ja-a-ha!

Little Daughter:

Umaya—ima,
Ha-ja-ja!
I'm easy to make jealous,
quick to rage!
Here I stand,
forgetting my poor songs.

But listen, cousin:
you're too eager
to deride me in your song;
let's pay a visit
to the people by the sand.
There I'll make an answer
to your clumsy mockery!

The company rises, and goes down to the village by the sand. On the way,
The Pearl sings:

I'll have no mercy
for the people by the sand:
they won't be friends of yours for long.
I'll show them
what you girls are really like:
all smiles outside,
but unchaste underneath,
willing to fuck casually with men,
and then give birth
in secret in the hills.
Do I lie or speak the truth?
I often envy
folk who slept at night
in ignorance of what went on.
Chaste people don't see anything.
But there are those who say
that you, too, secretly gave birth.
Do I lie or speak the truth?

At this, Little Daughter bursts into tears. And now The Pearl has an idea:

Let's sing,
let's go and see the people by the sand!
We'll open Little Daughter's sewing-box,
mess it up, reveal
her secrets!
Catch hold of Little Daughter, friends!

They grab her, and hold on to her, while The Pearl continues singing:

> The festival unites us,
> draws us close!
> Twist her loins,
> rock her hips!

And they force Little Daughter to dance, while The Pearl goes on singing:

> We'll ruthlessly reveal,
> her hidden thoughts!
> Together we'll expose her:
> she who always coveted my man.
> My anger, cousin, has arrived!

They reach the village. But here The Pearl's husband unexpectedly leaps
forward into the circle and sings:

> Now *my* anger wakes!
> Do you hear! Do you hear!
> I'm feeling like a fight!
> Do you hear! Do you hear!
> Let's break into the house,
> upset the piss-pot,
> tear the membrane window out,
> chuck the lamp on the shit-heap,
> let the boiled meat follow suit!
> Destroy, destroy the racks
> of meat and skins!
> I'm ready for a fight:
> I'm hot with rage,
> I'm hot for song, for song!
>
> Look, here's this wretched girl
> I had my fun with.
> Like animals in heat we were,
> when we went walking in the hills.

Oh, I remember how we hid
up on the Great Lichen mountain,
that sweet playground
for male animals!
Wagging our tails,
we looked out on
the sunny country of the south,
while we threw ourselves
down into the heather . . .

But what is happening?
Will no-one answer me?
Then shut your mouths!
We're going home,
and you can rest.
Daylight envelops the mountain.
Dawn has taken over from the night.

IV: CHARMS

NETSIT
(Copper Eskimo man, Musk Ox Folk)

Invocation

Spirit of the air,
come down,
come down!
Your shaman calls!

Spirit of the air
come down,
come down,
bite bad luck to death!

I rise,
I rise among spirits,
I see the phantoms of the dead!

Child, great child,
child-master of the air,
come down,
great infant spirit!

TATILGAK
(Copper Eskimo man, Musk Ox Folk)

Charm for Seal Blubber

Spirit of the air,
I call, I call!
I hiccup throaty sounds
which come from my inside.
Here I stand,
and shout my songs up
by my little hut.
Spirit of the air,
I call, I call!
Send me blubber
as you used to,
send me blubber
as you used to,
send me blubber!

PADLOQ
(Iglulik Eskimo man)

The Uncertain Life

To be spoken when suddenly in mortal danger

See, great earth,
these heaps
of pale bones in the wind!

They crumble in the air
of the wide world,
in the wide world's air,
pale, wind-dried bones,
decaying in the air!

ORPINGALIK
(Netsilik Eskimo man)

Lure

These words are to be spoken when the hunter has travelled away from the village, and has reached a place where he expects to find game. The charm will bring him luck in hunting reindeer.

Reindeer,
earth-louse,
long-legged,
large-eared,
bristly-neck,
don't run away
from me!
If I kill you,
I will offer
handsome presents
to your soul:
hides for kamiks,
moss for wicks.
Come happily,
towards me!
Come!

Greeting to Day

To be spoken from bed, in the early morning, before anybody has risen.

I will rise from sleep
with the swiftness
of the raven's wingbeat.
I will rise to meet the day.
Wa-wa.

My face turns
from the darkness,
my eyes turn to meet
the dawn, whitening the sky.

NAKASUK
(Netsilik Eskimo man)

Prayer for Strength

I am a man.
A bracelet, strong
as the word Yes,
clasps me.
The Yes-word's bracelet
brings me strength.
Aija-ija!

Little gull, high in the air,
fly down to me,
settle on my shoulder,
rest in the hollow of my palm!

Little gull, high in the air,
splitting the wind,
fly down to me,
fly down to me!

Your wings glow
up there in the red cold!
Give me strength!

EAST GREENLAND
(From Angmagssalik)

Magic Words to Clear the Fog

Ja-ia
It's not from me,
the steam that's rising,
it's not from me
the steam that's rising!
Ja-ia.

It's the river-people
steaming!
It's the river-people
steaming!
Ja-ia.

Let the fog
drift out to sea,
and sink
in the horizon!
Ja-ia.

Ija-ija,
a furious storm
surrounds me,
  ija-ija!
But quiet and glossy
lies the sea,
  ija-ija!
The spirit of the air
smooths my path,
  ija-ija!
I paddle on
in quiet water,
out of danger.
  Ija-ija!

Prayer for Heat

A charm to be spoken over a new hut before taking up residence.

Look! Look! Look!
  A fire!
Ija-ija,
  burning fire,
bright and hot!
  Ija-ija,
fire up there!
  Fire inside!
Fire! Fire!

Afterword

There was once an old Eskimo named Satdlagé : an ordinary and modest man who attracted no particular attention except for the fact that he always remained silent when the villagers gathered at song-festivals to apostrophise the country or their fellow-men. This was in the days when everyone had his own songs which he performed with a chorus of women : when he praised all he found beautiful or condemned what had outraged him. No one found it impossible to compose. Only Satdlagé never opened his mouth. One evening when someone asked him why he never joined the singers, he told the following story :

"Once, when I was quite a young man, I wanted to compose a song about my village, and for a whole winter evening, I walked up and down in the moonlight, trying to fit words together which would go with a tune I was humming. I did find the words : excellent words which would convey to my friends the beauty of the mountains, and every delightful thing I saw when I went outside and opened my eyes. Pacing up and down on the frozen snow, I became so preoccupied with my thoughts that I quite forgot where I was. Suddenly I stop and lift my head. And look ! In front of me, the mountain near our village rises higher and steeper than I have ever seen it. It was almost as if it was very slowly growing out of the earth and coming to lean over me : dangerous and threatening. It was then that I heard a voice coming from the air : 'Little man !' it cried. 'The echo of your words has reached me ! Do you really think I can be contained in your song?' I was so frightened that I almost fell over backwards, and in the same moment, all the words I had put together in my song fled from my mind, and I ran home as fast as I could and hid in my hut. Ever since then I have never attempted to put words together. I had become afraid."

*   *   *

The above narrative conveys an unsophisticated man's view of the difficult and holy "vocation" of Eskimo song. And embracing its simplicity, I have attempted in this book to create an echo of these strange and unspoilt voices. On all the voyages I made, in which I aimed at fathoming the Eskimo mind, I came to realise that he is something very much more than the blood-thirsty hunter whose joy is at its highest when he kills his game and eats its meat. His stone-age harshness is only a shell; you don't have to penetrate far before you meet the essential purity of ancient man : a purity which is demonstrated by the foregoing pages. The Eskimo has a humility in the face of the pressures of life which springs from an innocence for which we must surely envy him, a humility which is demonstrated not only in the face of all the factors he must fear as being enemies of his welfare, but also when it comes to what he must see as being a source of happiness in life. These songs are the proof that an Eskimo's joy does not always express itself in noisy animalistic orgies of food as many people think. Can one imagine a more noble pastime than the exercise of verbal skill which is cultivated by these men and women —this labour to create beauty and harmony with which to render the language more rich—or this laborious mulling over of expressions to describe joy or sorrow, longing, impotence, mockery or humour? The joy these people feel in the power, the warmth and the hurt of words has never ceased to impress me. And the more I realised that a hard life in harsh surroundings necessarily leads to an emphasis on materialism, the more I marvelled at finding such an abundance of soul among them that singing and the composition of poetry had become an absolute necessity.

*   *   *

I shall never forget the extraordinary fascination of my first nights at the song-festivals in Northern Greenland. Inside the little huts the oil-lamps cast a hot and yellow light over the many half-naked bodies covering the floor and benches. There was a smell of raw meat and sweat—but only until the songs began. Then you forgot your surroundings and just listened. The longer the singing continued, the harder you concentrated. Eventually my astonishment was transformed into a feeling of natural solidarity with the performers and what they were singing. Despite the strangeness of the language, this was not foreign at all : there were notes and harmonies we recognised and which came to us like distant memories. Listen :

O, warmth of summer
gliding over the land in waves!
Not a gust of wind,
not a cloud—
And in the mountains,
the belling reindeer,
the sweet reindeer
in the bluish distance!
O, how it pulls me,
O, how it fills me with delight!
Sobbing with emotion,
I lie down on the earth.

*   *   *

Nor shall I ever forget that night in Cape Dan, not far from Ang-magssalik. They arrived, singing in a "wife-boat"—a whole company of happy people who had been invited to a song-festival at our village. We had waited for them impatiently all day, and had climbed the mountain several times to look out over the glossy fjord where the solid ice glittered. But no shout had heralded the arrival of our guests. The sun set, and after a short dusk, the moon came out. Then, just as the big red evening star rose calm and sparkling over the mountains, we heard the first voices from the sea, and we stood quietly and listened to them from the shore. We couldn't see anything, but we heard a song rise out of the fjord towards the mountainous coast, and long before we could discern the phosphorescence of the oars, we became engulfed in the emotion which was drifting towards us like a breeze. It was a chorus, led by old, cheerful women, and their worn voices, carrying the song, were mingled with a few deep male voices from the accompanying kayaks.

Our visitors were on the whole, elderly men and women : but they were doubly welcome, and a great village-house stood warm and lit up, ready to receive them all. We were not far from being a hundred souls in the tightly-packed crowd. The women had to undress so as to have enough room on the main bench, while the men filled the side benches along the walls. Seal-skins had been spread over the floor, on which people were lying in layers. The host, whose nick-name was The Child regretted that his house was smaller than his hospitality. The reason he had gathered so many people was that he wanted to show the strangers a song-festival typical of East Green-land. But before the songs started, we were to eat. Earlier that day, a provisions-trench had been opened. Now some young people were sent out, and presently a line was thrown through the corridor into the room we were in. The people standing nearest started pulling at the rope, and a killer-seal—whole, not skinned, with hair and all—rolled onto the floor. The serving of 700 lb of food was as informal as its preparation. Blubber and meat were handed out to guests until it was all gone, and what you couldn't finish on the spot, you were allowed to take home with you. There was plenty to go round, so nobody had to behave greedily. We talked cheerfully and ate our fill—yet the predominant feeling was that this was only the beginning.

As soon as the meal was over, the host jumped onto the floor and positioned himself in the space reserved for the performers. Holding the magic drum, he looked round his circle of guests with satisfaction. Then, drumming slowly, he began to twist his body in dance, opening the evening with a solemn song with no other words than "awaija-awaija", which was immediately taken up by the great chorus.

Eskimo song has its roots in religion. Man has learned how to express his feelings with tunes which in the early days of the world came to him from giants and spirits which lived inland and among the mountains. The shaman, returning from his solitary quest for wisdom would bring these tunes to the villages and pass them on to man. All song is therefore holy. Dance was regarded as a secular, but festive addition.

* * *

As soon as the first song was over, another man seized the drum. This was Kilimê, the oldest member of the tribe, who had survived from the days when everyone was heathen. He had long grizzled hair which fluttered wildly around his face when he began his dance. He wanted to perform a fighting-song, a song of derision he had composed in his youth, when all dispute was resolved in song : and he beat his drum with the force of a youth and sang the song about the abduction which is given earlier in this book. An imaginary adversary was put in front of him, whom he hovered over like an eagle, descending without warning with hissing noises and nasal snorts, butting at the head with his hardened skull. All the while, he beat the drum and screamed out the words of his song. In the old days, butting-practice for the song contest was no joke. You tied the skull of a seal to a post, and exercised your forehead, temples and eyebrows against it. Many a broken nose has been the beginning of a friendship which received its baptism in this kind of duel.

After Kilimê, a couple of women had their turn. They normally lived in modest submission on the side-bench, but tonight they had command of everyone's attention. They delved into their past experience and came up with a song about their youth. They were bald and rheumatic in their old age, but men had once duelled for them in song-contests, and fought for the honour of giving them brilliant feasting-clothes. Their minds had once been filled with the love of life and jealousies; and now, as they performed, they touched on chords which had the resonance of distant wisdom and experience, never making themselves ridiculous, in spite of their rusty voices.

The feast continued in a continuous series of baroque and imaginative happenings. One man was suddenly noticed flat out on the floor, moving his head up and down, and singing. He was engaged in an animal pantomime, and was pretending to be a whale. His song described the life of the whale, and as he glided over the floor, he sucked up water from the container and blew it out over the nearest naked women. Drum-beats, laughter and shouts followed in the wake of the performer. The floor seemed to grow; it was endowed with distant horizons; the sea was licking the foot of the bench . . .

The whole village had turned out to the feast, and it was to last until the morning sun shone through the window-pane of gut, which was frosted now with flowers of ice.

*　　　*　　　*

Other images from other districts and of other Eskimos glide past me. I shall select only one of them, and describe what I remember of the Musk Ox Folk: the finest Eskimo singers I ever met.

I had been travelling by sleigh with the young Netsit, and it was a long time since we had seen any human beings. One afternoon, as dusk was falling, we suddenly round a small promontory and find ourselves in the middle of a village. It was one of the largest I had visited. More than thirty igloos had been built close together on a slope, and in the middle of this complex, the feasting-house raised its brilliant dome above the other snowy roofs: a temple to joy in the middle of one of the great snow-drifts of the waste-land.

The Canadian tribes who will soon be the only Eskimos to cultivate the heathen song-festivals, always built a special feasting-house called the *qagshé* They spend their time singing in the *qagshé* when meat is plentiful. Our village had just completed the great autumn reindeer-hunts and there was an abundance of provisions. We were offered tremendous meals in all the igloos we managed to visit, and then in the evening were invited to the *qagshé* for dancing and singing.

The *qagshé* was a vast hall, constructed with enormous blocks of snow, which could easily accommodate 60 people for a feast or a gathering. So as to make it warm and cosy even in the middle of the day, two rather effective wings had been added, which gave on to the large room in which the assembly took place. Both wings were occupied. In one, a young mother on the side-bench nursed two infants who were continually trying to get at her sewing. Her big stone wall-lamp radiated light and warmth into the room, and you couldn't help admiring the comfort provided by the beautiful reindeer-fur rugs which covered the bench. Arctic cod, salmon and dried meat were piled up on the bench, indicating to everyone that it was open house to all who wanted a bite to eat. In the opposite wing, the side-bench was also occupied, and equipped in exactly the same way, but the couple who usually sat there had joined the chorus for the evening, and some young girls who had made themselves responsible for looking after the lamp were standing on the bench looking on with much curiosity.

In the hollow dome of the hall, some niches had been carved out of the snow-blocks, and small oil-lamps were burning in these, throwing an unearthly light over the men and women who made up the chorus. They were standing in a circle round the principle singer who was in the middle of the hall with an enormous drum in his hand. This drum is so large that often whole reindeer-hides are needed to cover it; the wooden frame onto which the hides are stretched must consequently be very sturdy, and therefore the drum (which is held in the left hand) is extremely heavy. No wonder it requires both strength and training to perform with it for often several hours together.

Here, in the native country of the reindeer, both men and women dress in special dance-costumes, which are adorned with beautiful in-sets of white reindeer-belly fur. In addition, the men wear on their shoulders and backs skins of white ermine which flutter like flags when they move around. The needlework which goes into making the kamiks (boots) is also very carefully executed : and they are embroidered with white and red strips of skin. The head is crowned with a cap, made from the skin of a diver with the beak pointing upwards like the spike of a helmet. The dancer-drummer who is standing in the middle of the crowd also acts as the principle singer. He starts the appropriate song, and not until he has sung a certain amount does the chorus join in. Then deep male voices blend with high shrill sopranos. From the very first, the tunes are riveting and carry us away. It was men such as Tatilgak, Heq, Netsit and King-merut who were singing, and their compositions are reproduced above. And now, when I remember the inexplicable way in which words, music and dance mingled into one great wave of feeling that lifted us up and for a moment made us forget everything else, I can understand more clearly than ever, how difficult it is to take the songs of the Eskimos out of their own context. For the words of the songs are only part of the whole intended effect. Read an opera libretto without music, staging and performers, and you have a comparison.

*   *   *

This anthology, then, is a small selection of the songs which, over the years, I have heard and written down on my voyages among the Eskimos. Most of them date from the Fifth Thule Expedition, and those who may be interested in a wider selection are directed to the scientific publications of the expedition, where all the material (will) appear in the Eskimo dialects with English translation. In the present anthology the first section contains a variety of songs of mood, and in the second section there are examples of hunting-songs. These latter are difficult to separate from the songs of mood as so many of the songs touch on game, and the joys and disappointments of the hunter. Then come the songs of derision, which are fundamental to the public justice of the Eskimo. If two men or two women fall out (even to the extent of becoming mortal enemies) the quarrel can be resolved in song-contest. The two adversaries summon their friends to act as witnesses, and then they have their reckoning. All the spectators at a song-contest arrive festively clad, in clothes which have never been worn before. The challenge must be issued some time before the event, so that the adversary may prepare his answer, defence or counter-attack. The enemies stand in the middle of the floor, surrounded by spectators. The challenger must speak first, and he dances and beats the drum as he sings. The one who succeeds best in ridiculing his opponent is jubilantly declared victorious. However, words are not the only weapon. The Canadian Eskimos combined boxing with their songs, while in East Greenland, blows with the head were dealt with such violence, that a man's eyes would often swell and quite close up. A return bout came another evening : during the whole of a song the "recipient" had to stand smiling and take both mockery and beating without showing they affected him at all. When eventually everything had been fought out, old grudges were usually forgotten, and the combatants became such good friends that they swapped wives and exchanged gifts as tokens of reconcilation. The charms in the fourth section are not poems or songs in the same sense as the others. They are old mysterious combinations of words which have been handed down from time immemorial. They must only be owned and used by the person they are to assist : for if they become common knowledge, they lose their power to bestow luck in hunting, to heal sickness, to bring about good weather or snow fit to drive a sleigh on, or whatever they may be meant for. They are included in this collection for their sparse "to-the-point" language which conveys so beautifully the wish that is being expressed.

Incidentally, the Eskimos hardly ever sing or perform the songs of others. Every man and woman, sometimes even children, has his own poems : and this despite the fact that it is justifiably regarded as a large-scale and difficult task to create a good new song. They labour with words and expressions to a much higher degree than one would have credited a "primitive" hunting-people. Each poem must match its tune. The tune often contains intervals which do not occur in our system of harmony; and rhythmically, it becomes so complicated that a Westerner only comprehends it with extreme difficulty. At first, its apparent monotony makes it difficult to distinguish one tune from another, and you think they are all the same. This however, is not the case. Even if the difference is small, each song has its own definite variations which it is not easy to grasp, because the text isn't contained by any sort of metrical regularity. Rhyme isn't known, but there are plenty of other factors to observe : the words have to be co-ordinated with the regular accompaniment of the drum; and the dance must be done according to strictly observed rules. All this must be taken into consideration while the song is being composed. When at last the day comes for the poet to appear before his fellow villagers, it is absolutely necessary that he masters his technique so well that the chorus will know immediately when to fall in with him, and lend support to his song and tempo. I have nothing but admiration for these poets who had to be dancers, drummers, singers, chorus-masters without being first able to transcribe their inspiration onto a patient piece of paper, where everything could be more closely valued, worked on and improved, until it became the way they wanted it to be.

The Eskimo has no written language to assist him, and consequently poetry-writing is a slow and laborious exercise of memory. No wonder then that they always seek solitude in which to compose. Pacing up and down on the top of a mountain, with a view over the country, or on a broad plain—sometimes day after day—the poet tries to build up his song, quietly mumbling the phrases as he works. It is not easy to memorise all the words that sound well and harmonise. Phrase after phrase must be repeated and spontaneous thoughts seized on and secured, until the song has at last been firmly memorised. No wonder then, that the Eskimo composes his poetry in a spirit of humility : he realises how narrow a road it is to the top. On the other hand, he understands fully how to enjoy the ecstasy of creation when the first birth-pangs are over.

It's perhaps superfluous to point out that it hasn't been an easy task translating these poems into Danish. The difficulty lay in the thousands of years' difference between our languages and cultures. Whatever I did, I finally lacked all the things that gave the songs life in their country of origin. How could I recreate the sound of the drum—whether resonantly festive, noisy and defiant or softly lamenting—let alone the choruses which would rise and continue rising until the ecstasy suddenly beat them down into the hushed hissing of the spirit songs—those choruses which are to the song as breath which runs back and forth in the human throat?

Here I was with my neat written language and my sober orthography, and a feeling that I couldn't bestow sufficient form or force to the cries of joy or fear of these unlettered people. All I can say about my work is that I have attempted conscientiously to preserve the spirit of the poems as well as making an effort to imitate the irregularity of the words, rhythms, sounds and everything that was intended to show transitions in the text and melody. To give some idea of my method, I have, at the end of the book, reproduced some Eskimo originals with a literal translation which can easily be compared to the final form of the poem.

*   *   *

So let *Snehyttens Sange* be left to its fate. These songs don't arrive like fragile orchids from the hot-houses of professional poets; they have flowered like rough, weather-beaten saxifrage which has taken root on rock. And they ought to matter to us. For do we not hear through them something that reminds us of the original features of our own old songs—the same life-giving warmth, the same teasing humour, the same quiet melancholia—and sometimes in glimpses, a simple but grandiose pathos which grips us by virtue of its immediacy. Here is what the East Greenlander, Kilimê says :

"All songs are born to man out in the great wastes. Sometimes they come to us like weeping, deep from the pangs of the heart, sometimes like a playful laughter which springs from the joy that life and the wonderful expanses of the world around us provide. We do not know how songs arrive with our breath—in the form of words and music, and not as ordinary speech—and then become the property of the person who understands how to sing to others."

KNUD RASMUSSEN
October 1930

NOTES

i. THE COPPER ESKIMOS

In 1923, accompanied by Netsit ("The Seal"), Rasmussen visited a "notoriously dangerous" Copper Eskimo group, the Kiluhigtormiut ("The People at the Head of the Deep Fjord"). It was there that the song-festival described in the Afterword (pp. 103–5) took place. The following passage is an abbreviated account (from *Report of the Fifth Trade Expedition*) of Rasmussen's arrival at the village.

The village is smoking—the snow huts are stove-heated and the smoke of burning twigs ascends our nostrils. On every snow roof a chimney sticks out brutally, out of all congruity with the style and idea of the snow hut, but picturesque and comforting to one who is starving with cold.

Sealing has not yet started, and therefore they are using sheet iron stoves with twigs, a habit they have learned of the Indians who live in the interior not far away. To me, unprepared for it as I am and accustomed to the modest little blubber lamp of the snow hut it is crude and yet cosy.

Smoke, thin, white smoke and the scent of the forest from every single snow house! And yet, how I am gripped by it, this sign of home and indoor warmth.

For many months we have only been used to finding villages consisting of a few huts, and half a score of people were a crowd. Now a shout of joy sounds over the whole of this metropolis; every snow orifice emits human beings, and soon I am the centre of a cascade of laughter, exclamation and question.

Lively people, even presumptuous, but good-natured at heart. Savage in manner, but sensitive to a quick and cutting word. Then mildly venturing, to see how far they can go, but withdrawing good-humouredly when parried. The Eskimos here are not the peaceful, rather shy people we know in Greenland. They are people who want to mix witn all, white men too, without ceremony. And when, as in my case, they get the chance of having him alone, they like to tease him as we often do with dangerous beasts behind the bars of a cage.

One tries to take the pipe out of my mouth—Ow! He won't try that again. Another pulls my short coat tail—a Cape York model— Oh! Surely that was a mistake! And when I unload and start to feed my dogs, they all want blubber. The women step forward and ask for it, for sealing has not yet begun and they are all hungry for delicacies and wild for a piece of the lovely fresh frozen pink blubber. But I answer them :

"Do you think I have come all this way to feed you with blubber? It is for my dogs, and there are men enough here. Go out on to the ice and start hunting at the breathing holes if you want blubber!"

A laugh goes all round.

I stand quite alone amid the crowd; for my companion Netsit is himself a native of the place and simply laughs at the others' amusement and all their impudent jesting.

"Who are you? Are you a trader, come for foxes?"

"I have come here to see you and find out what you are made of."

Shouts of laughter!

An elderly man answers, a little at sea because he does not know whether I am serious or not : "Hey! You'll see many kinds of people here. Some are pretty, but most of them are ugly, and you'll not get much pleasure out of their faces."

I am tickled at all this crude impudence, and yet it seems for a moment that their eagerness is cooling down a little. I must do something to show that I do not fear them at all, and so I sling out :

"I have come to you trustingly, though your reputation is none of the best. It is not many years since two white men were killed on this spot, and the police are not flattering in their description of you. But you see, I am not afraid to meet you alone."

With these words I point over to a smiling little valley between two high mountains quite close to the village, the place where the two members of an American expedition were murdered a few years back.[1]

"We didn't do it, it was the white men themselves who picked a quarrel. We are a good-natured people, but high spirited. We are fond of song and laughter and never think of doing harm as long

---

[1] Two American scientists, Radford and Street, in 1913 had made a sledge journey across the Barren Grounds to the Arctic Coast. At the head of Bathurst Inlet, where they wished to obtain helpers for the rest of their journey westwards, they had a quarrel with the natives, and this quarrel ended in their being stabbed to death by the men of the village. Radford is described as a fiery-tempered man who had whipped the Eskimo who would not accompany them, and so he undoubtedly had himself to blame for what happened (*Report of the Fifth Thule Expedition*, Vol. 9).

as we have nothing to fear. You are our friend and have nothing to be afraid of."

Thus the murder-band.

I am conducted into a snow hut which will be our quarters for the present. Our hostess is Qernertoq, "the black one". She receives both "The Seal"[2] and myself with marked signs of hospitality, and yet I learn later that her husband was killed by "The Seal's" father, who was then killed by her father. But this is a little private matter that does not seem to be an obstacle to sociability.

I had been brusque, in order to keep them at a distance, hard and stern; but now a woman came to me, took hold of my shoulder, looked straight into my eyes and said:

"Tell me, stranger, are you a man whom a woman can make to smile?"

I had to laugh aloud. My friendship with my neighbours was sealed.

That first afternoon I spent going from house to house, calling on people. They were all large and light snow huts, but there was no Eskimo air about them on account of the iron stoves and the long pipes that ran out through the melted roof. The crackling fires radiated tremendous heat, and yet the snow roof round the fire place was so cleverly constructed that there was scarcely any drip. Here and there were holes, it is true, but the draught coming in through these openings was pleasant if anything.

Every house was full, not only of people but of dogs too; it seemed that nobody had the heart to deny them the warmth. They were mostly big dogs, in good condition and having a splendid, newly cast winter coat.

I paid my calls accompanied by two young women who always seemed to be together, and seemed to have the idea that I should complete my circle of acquaintances in the course of one afternoon. They were taller than the others, and prettier, and, with their long braided hair, which in front fell over temples and cheeks in profusion, looked more like Indian girls than Eskimos. Their complexion was fair and delicate, and about their faces there was that blondeness that is so characteristic of many of the Eskimos in these parts.

We terminated our visits at the house of Quersoq, "cough", and his wife Uviloq, "mussel"; they sat side by side on the platform,

---

[2] I.e. Netsit, Rasmussen's guide—a man of about twenty-five who, in addition to singing the five songs translated at the beginning of this book, transmitted a large number of folk-tales which are printed in *Report of the Fifth Thule Expedition*, Vol. 9.

their bearing radiating pleasure and well-being so obviously that I could not help recollecting that here I was face to face with a man who once tried to shoot himself because his wife "was unbearable". I counted twelve dogs in their house, and as neighbours were there too, sharing the evening meal, these dogs kept host and hostess in a constant state of excitement. They were everywhere, just where they were most in the way, and were not above trying to snap a fish or bite of meat out of the hands of the guests.

There were twenty-five people in the house, apparently the youth of the village for the most part, all being fed on frozen salmon and dried caribou meat; nevertheless I discovered an old man away in a corner, Kataluk by name, who obviously had only come there to eat. The noisy company did not seem to concern him in the slightest, and he consumed everything that came near him with badly concealed eagerness.

SONGS OF THE COPPER ESKIMOS

Every man, and most of the women, have their own songs with which they have been inspired and then composed themselves. Apart from these new songs, however, they have special spirit hymns, and these too are sung in the festival house when the mistress of the sea beasts, Arnakäpshâluk, is to be invoked. These hymns, which are called Aqiutit, have a simple solemnity about their melodies and they are directed to Hilap inue, the spirits of the air, who alone can help mankind. Both words and tunes are immensely old and are said to have been handed down from generation to generation. They have this in common with the ordinary magic songs that their words are often vague, but no one ever seeks to try to understand them; it is considered that they act by the very force of their fantasy and mysteriousness.

Finally, there is Ingulrait pise, or "the songs of the departed". These, too, have been handed down, and although a certain name may often be coupled with them, no one knows how old they really are. As a rule the modern songs are in glorification of some achievement, or some experience that has left its impression. In contrast to these "the songs of the departed" are much more sentimental and often seek to express some philosophy of life.

*　　　*　　　*

No especial grouping of the songs has been attempted; they are given in the order in which I myself received them. In fact, I believe that a classification that sharply differentiated between ancient songs, modern songs and spirit hymns would to some extent be arbitrary, as the real poets among the Umingmaktormiut undoubtedly set their mark upon the old songs by the personal form they unconsciously give them. It will suffice for me to say that never in any other single group, neither in Greenland, Canada nor Alaska, have I met such a poetically gifted people as the Musk Ox folk.

Every singer usually presents his song in two sections—two songs which most frequently have nothing to do with each other. The second section is called its puhuhauta; literally this means "that by means of which one knocks a hole through it", and is to be understood as a conclusion or continuation. Sometimes they say more directly uviua : its increase. Both words are used promiscuously.

In spite of his disclaimer, Rasmussen does provide some classification :

1. OLD SONGS
Hunger (Kingmerut)
Song about Reindeer, Musk Oxen, Women, etc. (Netsit)
Song of a Diffident Man (Qerraq)
Hymn to the Spirit of the Air (Igpakuhak)
Longing for Song Contest (Igpakuhak) [in *Snehyttens Sange,* Rasmussen classified this poem as a song of derision, and in our translations it will be found in that section. It is, however, an example of an unrelated second section of a two-part poem, and belongs to *Hymn to the Spirit of the Air.*]

2. SONGS OF THE DEPARTED ONES
Netsit explains the meaning of this as follows : very old people and dead people are called inerlrait : the departing, or the departed. Their songs are particularly popular. Sometimes they recall the name of the man who first sang them, but everything else about him has been forgotten beyond the fact that "he once lived in our land"; only his song is remembered and sung in the dance-house.
Men's Impotence (Netsit)
Where I wonder? [This is the concluding section to *Men's Impotence*]
A Forgotten Man's Song about the Winds (Tatilgak)
The Sun and the Moon and the Fear of Loneliness [In *Snehyttens*

Sange Rasmussen attributes this poem to Tatilgak. In *Report of the Fifth Thule Expedition,* Vol. 9, it is printed as the concluding song of "Ulipshialuk's wife", and follows a song by Ulupsialuk himself, which is not published in *Snehyttens Sange.*]

3. SPIRIT HYMNS

Invocation (Netsit) [The version in *Snehyttens Sange* appears to be a composite version of three shorter hymns, possibly sung in close succession.]

Bird Song (Tatilgak)

1. 25. "Does it have teeth?"—Rasmussen notes : Here is a reference to the fact that, unlike other birds, the raven is able to bite a thong through, and therefore it is jokingly asked if it has a "fang" (carnassial tooth), the teeth the dogs use to chew seal thongs when they eat them.

Charm for Seal Blubber (Tatilgak)

Sick Man's Song (Heq)

Spirit Song (Netsit)

When I asked Heq what they meant by singing a song that nobody understood, neither its substance nor hints, he answered : "the spirit hymns have to do with supernatural and unreal things, so ordinary people do not need to understand them. The wisdom in them is often concealed, and one must simply utter the words, which have a special power." Regarding the mysterious references to the woman, Heq gave the following explanation : because he usually looks for women's uncleanness and their breach of taboo and precepts, the sources of so many accidents and misfortunes to mankind. I.e., misfortunes were often attributed to breach of taboo which could not be traced, but were frequently supposed to derive from "unclean women" (menstruating, or in pre- or post-natal state) breaking eating prohibitions, etc.

Dead Man's Song

They say that Aijuk's song was dreamt by Paulinaq after his (Aijuk's) death. The dead are often interred by being left in the snow hut in which they have died, it being closed up with a block of snow.

The Widow's Song (Qernertoq)

The conclusion is vague. Its meaning is probably that all her relatives have gone, killed either by evil spirits or by man. All she has now is the protection her amulets give her.

Delight in Nature

This is the concluding section to Qivsarina's song about Aitaq, his father's second wife, dreamt by Heq. [As *Delight in Nature* is attributed to Tatilgak in *Snehyttens Sange*, and "Willow Twig" is a translation of the name Heq (supposedly himself the dreamer of this poem's first part), the authorship of this poem is in some doubt!]

Song about Reindeer, Musk Oxen, Women, and Men who want to Show Off, (Netsit, p. 5)
l. 16. "Crossing-place": Rasmussen notes that especially in the days when the natives had no fire-arms . . . all the hunting took place at the swimming places (i.e., water narrow enough for reindeer to negotiate), in kayaks and with spears or with bow and arrows from special hiding places called *talut*.
l. 33. "little men": The Eskimos frequently referred to themselves as such. (Cf. also *Hymn to the Spirit of the Air*.)

The song expresses Netsit's exuberance both as a hunter and as a poet. Survival depended on the hunting that took place during the seasonal migrations that he describes. A tragic and ironic consequence of the introduction of fire-arms to some Eskimo groups was such a wholesale slaughter of the reindeer, that the herds subsequently deviated from their traditional routes and the Eskimos no longer knew where to await them. To most Eskimos, however, the rifle became an indispensable weapon against starvation.

Charm for Seal Blubber (Tatilgak, p. 94)
Seven magic songs in addition to this charm were passed down to Tatilgak by his grandfather. They may only be used inside the house early in the morning, before anybody has set foot on the floor. On rare occasions, under special circumstances, they may be uttered under the open sky, but only in places where there are no tracks in the snow.

Tatilgak moreover gave the following explanation: one makes magic songs when a man's thoughts begin to turn towards another or something that does not concern him; without his hearing it, one makes magic songs so that there may be calm in his mind, to make his thoughts pleasant—for a man is dangerous when he is angry.
Report of the Fifth Thule Expedition, Vol. 9, Chapter 6

ii. THE IGLULIK ESKIMOS

(from *Report of the Fifth Thule Expedition*, Volume 7)

The Eskimo temperament finds a lively and characteristic expression in the mode of entertainment chosen as soon as but a few individuals are gathered together. The natural healthy joy of life must have an outlet, and this is found in boisterous games as well as in song and dance. Underlying all the games is the dominant passion of rivalry, always seeking to show who is best in various forms of activity: the swiftest, the strongest, the cleverest and most adroit. There are many different kinds of games, often in the form of gymnastic exercises, which are associated with the festivals invariably held when guests are to be entertained, and the party as a whole are otherwise fit and well, with meat enough for a banquet. There are ball games, races, trials of strength, boxing contests, archery etc.; but the same spirit of rivalry which makes all this kind of sport exciting, is also found in the song contests which are held in the feasting house as the culmination of all the merry items in the entertainment. And where there are several families living in one village, there is no need of visitors to provide the occasion, the party is then sufficient in itself. The autumn and the dark season naturally form the great time for song; as if it were desired to chase away the thoughts of the winter now inevitably approaching, in the course of which so much may happen in the way of unlooked for, undesirable events, if Sila[1] and the other guiding powers are not favourably disposed towards mankind.

The great song festivals at which I have been present during the dark season are the most original and the prettiest kind of pastime I have ever witnessed. Every man and every woman, sometimes also the children, will have his or her own songs, with appropriate melodies, which are sung in the qag·e, the great snow hut which is set up in every village where life and good spirits abound. Those taking part in a song festival are called qagi·ʃut; the poem recited is

[1] Spirit of the weather.

119

called pisɛq, the melody of a song iᵛŋɛrut: and to sing is iᵛŋɛrtaˑrnɛq; the combination of song, words and dance is expressed by the word mumɛrnɛq: "changing about"; having reference to the fact that as soon as the leading singer has finished, another comes forward: he sings: mumɛrpɔq, plural mumɛrtut. The chorus, which must always accompany the leading singer, who beats time with his drum while dancing, is called iɲiɔrtut: those who accompany in song.

A qagˑe is heated and lighted by one or more lamps; to make it thoroughly festive, there must be no lack of blubber, and that is one reason why it is difficult to celebrate these festivals unless there is abundance of everything. If the hunting has been such as to require economy, no special feasting house is built, but the whole community assemble in the largest house in the place. An essential preliminary to the success of the general entertainment is the careful practising of the songs by each family at home in their own huts. These people have no written characters, and no means of breaking the monotony of indoor life but what they can make for themselves, so that the songs are apt to be their chief method of entertainment. Where all are well, and have meat enough, everyone is cheerful and always ready to sing, consequently there is nearly always singing in every hut of an evening, before the family retire to rest. Each sits in his or her own usual place, the housewife with her needlework, the husband with his hunting implements, while one of the younger members takes the drum and beats time; all the rest then hum the melodies and try to fix the words in their minds.

When the song festivals are held in the qagˑe, the party assemble there every evening. Among villagers still living inland, because their womenfolk have not yet finished their needlework, the gathering begins early in the afternoon, and lasts until late in the evening, song and dance continuing uninterruptedly all the time. Should there happen to be visitors, the entertainment may last all night. The men who have most meat contribute the most delicious kinds of food, and the festival opens with a great banquet, at which everyone may eat as much as he can stuff.

Then, when the singing is to begin, the performers are drawn up in a circle, the men inside, the women outside. The one who is to lead off with an original composition now steps forward, holding the large drum or tambourine, called qilaut, a term possibly related to the qilavɔq previously mentioned: the art of getting into touch with spirits apart from the ordinary invocation. For qilaut means literally: "that by means of which the spirits are called up". This term for the drum, which with its mysterious rumbling dominates the general tone of the songs is doubtless a reminiscence of the time when all song was sacred. For the old ones believe that song came to man from the souls in the Land of the Dead, brought thence by a shaman; spirit songs are therefore the beginning of all song. And the direct relation of the songs to the spirits is also explained by the fact that every Eskimo who under the influence of powerful emotion loses control of himself, often breaks into song, whether the occasion be pleasurable or the reverse.

Compare here, the manner in which Aua the shaman could suddenly fall a prey to an inexplicable dread, burst into tears and sing the song of joy. Or the case of Uvavnuk, when struck by the meteor suddenly bursting into song over the theme of all that moved her and made her a shaman.

As a rule, each leading singer has to sing a certain number of songs, but not too many; three, for instance, and often it is so arranged that the one who comes after him must sing at least as many as the first. Should he fail to equal the number of his predecessor, he is accounted a poor singer, a man without experience or imagination. Before the song festival begins, the drum has to be carefully tuned up. The skin, which is stretched on a wooden frame sometimes quite round, sometimes oval in shape, is made from the hide of a caribou cow or calf with the hair removed. This is called ija·, the "eye" of the drum, and must be moistened with water and well stretched before use. Only thus will it give the true, mysterious rumbling and thundering sound.

The singer generally opens with a modest declaration to the effect that he cannot remember his insignificant songs. This is intended to suggest that he considers himself but a poor singer; the idea being, that the less one leads the audience to expect, the humbler one's estimation of one's own performance, the more likelihood there will be of producing a good effect. A conceited singer, who thinks himself a master of his art, has little power over his audience.

The singer stands in the middle of the floor, with knees slightly bent, the upper part of the body bowed slightly forward, swaying from the hips, and rising and sinking from the knees with a rhythmic movement, keeping time throughout with his own beating of the drum. Then he begins to sing, keeping his eyes shut all the time; for a singer and a poet must always look inward in thought, concentrating on his own emotion.

There are very precise rules for the use of the qilaut. The skin of the drum itself is never struck, the edge of the wooden frame being beaten instead, with a short and rather thick stick. The drum is held in the left hand, by a short handle attached to the frame, and as it is fairly heavy, and has to be constantly moved to and fro, it requires not only skill, but also considerable muscular power, to keep this going sometimes for hours on end. The singer's own movements, the beating of the drum, and the words of the song must fit in one with another according to certain definite rules, which appear easy and obvious to an onlooker, but anyone trying to imitate the performance will inevitably get out of time. It is a great art to keep one's attention fixed on the rhythmic movements of the body, the beats of the drum, which must accompany, yet not coincide with, the bending of the knees; then there is also the time of the melody itself, which must likewise follow the movements, and finally the words, which have to be remembered very accurately, with the inconceivably numerous repetitions recurring at certain particular parts of the song. And the singer, while keeping all this in mind, must at the same time inspire his chorus so that it is led up to that ecstasy which can at times carry a simple melody for hours, supported only by a refrain consisting of ajaja, ajaja. I have been present at song festivals lasting for 14–16 hours, which shows what song means to these people. Imagine a concert in any civilised community lasting for that length of time! But the secret of the Eskimos' endurance lies of course in the fact that they are simple and primitive natures, working themselves up collectively into an ecstasy which makes them forget all else.

I have many a time endeavoured to learn their songs so as to be able myself to take part in a performance at the qag·e, but with no great success. I never found any difficulty in making up a song that should fulfil the ordinary requirements, though it was not easy to equal the natural primitive temperament in its power of finding simple and yet poetic forms of expression; but as soon as I tried to accompany myself on the drum, with the very precise movements of the body that go with it, I invariably got out of time, and thus lost my grip of those whom it was my business to inspire as my chorus. These attempts of my own to take part gave me an increased respect for this particular form of the art of singing, and now that I have to describe, as far as I can, the performance as a whole, I can only say that the general feeling, the emotional atmosphere in a qag·e among men and women enlivened by song is something that cannot be conveyed save by actual experience. Some slight idea of it may perhaps be given some day, when the "talking film" has attained a higher degree of technical perfection—if it gets there in time it would then have to be by a combination of the songs in the Eskimo tongue and the dancing in living pictures. Unfortunately, I was unable to record their melodies on the phonograph, as our instrument was out of order. I hope then at some future date to be able to revert to this complicated but humanly speaking highly interesting subject; for the present, I must confine myself to the Eskimos' own view.

There are various kinds of songs. Firstly those inspired originally by some great joy or sorrow, in a word, an emotion so powerful that it cannot find vent in ordinary everyday language. Then there are songs merely intended to give the joy of life, of hunting, rejoicing in the beasts of the chase, and all the good and ill that man can experience when among his fellow men. Then again, every man who aspires to be considered one with any power of gathering his neighbours together must also have challenged some one else to a song contest; and in this he must have his own particular rival, one whom he delights to compete with, either in the beauty of his songs as such, or in the skilful composition and delivery of metrical abuse. He describes the experiences which he considers most out of the ordinary, and best calculated to impress others with the idea of his own prowess as a hunter and courage as a man. Two such opponents in song contests must be the very best of friends; they call themselves, indeed, iglɔre·k, which means "song cousins", and must endeavour, not only in their verses but also in all manner of sport, each to outdo the other; when they meet, they must exchange costly gifts, here also endeavouring each to surpass the other in extravagant generosity. Song cousins regard themselves as so intimately associated that whenever they meet, they change wives for the duration of their stay. On first meeting after a prolonged absence, they must embrace and kiss each other by rubbing noses.

Song cousins may very well expose each other in their respective songs, and thus deliver home truths, but it must always be done in a humorous form, and in words so chosen as to excite no feeling among the audience but that of merriment.

These cheerful duels of song must not be confused with those songs of abuse which, albeit cast in humorous form for greater effect, have nevertheless an entirely different background in the insolence with which the singer here endeavours to present his opponent in a ludicrous light and hold him up to derision. Such songs always originate in some old grudge or unsettled dispute, some incautious criticism, some words or action felt as an insult, and perhaps breaking up an old friendship. The only means then of restoring amicable relations is by vilifying each other in song before the whole community assembled in the qag·e. Here, no mercy must be shown; it is indeed considered manly to expose another's weakness with the utmost sharpness and severity; but behind all such castigation there must be a touch of humour, for mere abuse in itself is barren, and cannot bring about any reconciliation. It is legitimate to "be nasty", but one must be amusing at the same time, so as to make the audience laugh; and the one who can thus silence his opponent amid the laughter of the whole assembly, is the victor, and has put an end to the unfriendly feeling. Manly rivals must, as soon as they have given vent to their feelings, whether they lose or win, regard their quarrel as a thing of the past, and once more become good friends, exhanging valuable presents to celebrate the reconciliation. Sometimes the songs are accompanied by a kind of boxing, the parties striking each other with their fists, first on the shoulders, then in the face, not as a fight, but only to test each other's endurance and power of controlling emotion despite the pain. This form of boxing, which is called tiklu·t·ut, is well known among the Aivilingmiut and Iglulingmiut, but is especially prevalent among the Netsilingmiut.

Shamanism; Uvavnuk's enlightenment; her poem, Moved (*page* 27)
The first thing a shaman has to do when he has called up his helping spirits is to withdraw the soul from his pupil's eyes, brain and entrails. This is effected in a manner which cannot be explained, but every capable instructor must have the power of liberating the soul of eyes, brain and entrails from the pupil's body and handing it over to those helping spirits which will be at the disposal of the pupil himself when fully trained. Thus the helping spirits in question become familiarised with what is highest and noblest in the shaman-to-be; they get used to the sight of him, and will not be afraid when he afterwards invokes them himself.

The next thing an old shaman has to do for his pupil is to procure him an aŋak·ua by which is meant his "angákoq" i.e. the altogether special and particular element which makes this man an angákoq (shaman). It is also called his qaumanᴇq, his "lighting" or "enlightenment", for aŋak·ua consists of a mysterious light which the shaman suddenly feels in his body, inside his head, within the brain, an inexplicable searchlight, a luminous fire, which enables him to see in the dark, both literally and metaphorically speaking, for he can now, even, with closed eyes, see through darkness and perceive things and coming events which are hidden from others; thus they look into the future and into the secrets of others.

The first time a young shaman experiences this light, while sitting up on the bench invoking his helping spirits, it is as if the house in which he is suddenly rises; he sees far ahead of him, through mountains, exactly as if the earth were one great plain, and his eyes could reach to the end of the earth. Nothing is hidden from him any longer; not only can he see things far, far away but he can also discover souls, stolen souls, which are either kept concealed in far, strange lands or have been taken up or down to the Land of the Dead.

An aŋak·ua or qaumanᴇq is a faculty which the old shamans procure for their pupils from the Spirit of the Moon. There are also some who obtain it through the medium of some deceased person among the Udlormiut who is particularly fond of the pupil in question. Or again, it can be obtained through bears which appear in human form; bears in human form are the shamans' best helpers. And finally, it can also be obtained from the Mother of the Caribou, who lives far up inland, and is here called Pakitsumánga.

Uvavnuk is struck by a ball of fire

Uvavnuk had gone outside the hut one winter evening to make water. It was particularly dark that evening, as the moon was not visible. Then suddenly there appeared a glowing ball of fire in the sky, and it came rushing down to earth straight towards her. She would have got up and fled, but before she could pull up her breeches, the ball of fire struck her and entered into her. At the same moment she perceived that all within her grew light, and she lost consciousness. But from that moment also she became a great shaman. She had never before concerned herself with the invocation of spirits, but now iŋnᴇru·jäp inua, the spirit of the meteor, had entered into her and made her a shaman. She saw the spirit just before she fainted. It had two kinds of bodies, that rushed all glowing through space; one side was a bear, the other was like a human being; the head was that of a human being with the tusks of a bear.

Uvavnuk had fallen down and lost consciousness, but she got up again, and without knowing what she was doing, came running into the house; she came into the house singing: naluʃa·ruᵬlune tamai-salo patsisaialᴇrluɡit: there was nothing that was hidden from her now, and she began to reveal all the offences that had been committed by those in the house. Thus she purified them all.

Every shaman has his own particular song, which he sings when calling up his helping spirits; they must sing when the helping spirits enter into their bodies and speak with the voice of the helping spirits themselves. The song which Uvavnuk generally sang, and which she sang quite suddenly the first evening, without knowing why, after the meteor had struck her, was as follows:

"imʌrju·ble im·na
aulʌrjʌ·rmaŋa
iŋɛrajʌ·rmaŋa
ʌqajagin·ʌrmaŋa.
nʌ·rʒugʒu·p im·na
aulʌrjʌ·rmaŋa
iŋɛrajʌ·rmaŋa
aulagʌrinʌrmaŋa".

(Translation, page 27)

These two verses she repeated incessantly, aliaŋnʌrᵈlune i.e. in-toxicated with joy, so that all in the house felt the same intoxication of delight, alianaigusulɛrlutik, and without being asked, began to state all their misdeeds, as well as those of others, and those who felt themselves accused and admitted their offences obtained release from these by lifting their arms and making as if to fling away all evil; all that was false and wicked was thrown away. It was blown away as one blows a speck of dust from the hand:

"taiva·luk, taiva·luk: away with it, away with it!"

But there was this remarkable thing about Uvavnuk, that as soon as she came out of her trance, she no longer felt like a shaman; the light left her body and she was once more quite an ordinary person with no special powers. Only when the spirit of the meteor lit up the spirit light within her could she see and hear and know every-thing, and became at once a mighty magician. Shortly before her death she held a grand séance, and declared it was her wish that mankind should not suffer want, and she "manivai", i.e. brought forth from the interior of the earth all manner of game which she had obtained from Takánakapsâluk. This she declared, and after her death, the people of her village had a year of greater abundance in whale, walrus, seal and caribou than any had ever experienced before.

A Hunting Memory—Ivaluardjuk (page 25)
The best singers I met during our winters at Hudson's Bay were Aua and his brother Ivaluardjuk, whose most characteristic song I have already given in the introductory section. When sung, it pro-duced an altogether extraordinary effect on those present. And any-one who understands the Eskimo tongue will be able to appreciate the great power of expression and the elegance of form in the original text. For my own part, what impressed me most was the individuality of conception in the poet's endeavouring to further the

expression of his inspiration, or of his hunting experience, by lying down on the ice on a winter's day and in a vision recalling the contrast to the harshness of the moment in his fight with the gnats, which are the pests that accompany the delightful warmth of summer. The Eskimo poet does not mind if here and there some item be omitted in the chain of his associations; as long as he is sure of being understood, he is careful to avoid all weakening explanations. Here is the old man his limbs awry with the gout, shivering with cold one bitter winter's day, and, in order to give warmth to his description of a distant memory of the chase, he cries out into the driving snow:

> Cold and mosquitoes
> are torments
> that never come together.
> I lie down on the ice,
> I lie down on the ice and snow,
> so my jaws chatter.
> This is me!

This reference to the mosquitoes at once calls up recollections of summer in the minds of his hearers, and he drives them away again at once to bring forward the situation he has in view.

But when one tries to talk to one of these poets on the subject of poetry as an art, he will of course not understand in the least what we civilised people mean by the term. He will not admit that there is any special art associated with such productions, but at the most may grant it is a gift, and even then a gift which everyone should possess in some degree. I shall never forget Ivaluardjuk's astonishment and confusion when I tried to explain to him that in our country, there were people who devoted themselves exclusively to the production of poems and melodies. His first attempt at an explanation of this inconceivable suggestion was that such persons must be great shamans who had perhaps attained to some intimate relationship with the spirits, these then inspiring them continually with utterances of spiritual force. But as soon as he was informed that our poets were not shamans, merely people who handled words, thoughts and feelings according to the technique of a particular art, the problem appeared altogether beyond him. And it is precisely in this that we find the difference between the natural temperament of the uncultured native and the mind of more advanced humanity; between the Eskimo singer and the poet of any civilised race; the work of the latter being more a conscious attempt to create beauty and power in rhythm and rhyme. The word "inspiration", as we understand it, does not, of course, exist for the Eskimo; when he wishes to express anything corresponding to our conception of the term, he uses the simple phrase: "to feel emotion". But every normal human being must feel emotion at some time or other in the course of a lifetime, and thus all human beings are poets in the Eskimo sense of the word.

In order further to make clear Ivaluardjuk's ideas, I would once more refer to the woman Uvavnuk, who one dark night experienced her great emotion, the decisive inspiration of her life, through the medium of a meteor which came rushing down out of space and took up its abode in her, so that she, who had until then been quite an ordinary person, became clairvoyant, became a shaman, and could sing songs that had in themselves the warmth of the glowing meteor.

Finally, the Eskimo poet must—as far as I have been able to understand—in his spells of emotion, draw inspiration from the old spirit songs, which were the first songs mankind ever had; he must cry aloud to the empty air, shout incomprehensible, often meaningless words at the governing powers, yet withal words which are an attempt at a form of expression unlike that of everyday speech. Consequently, no one can become a poet who had not complete faith in the power of words. When I asked Ivaluardjuk about the power of words, he would smile shyly and answer that it was something no one could explain; for the rest, he would refer me to the old magic song I had already learned, and which made all difficult things easy. Or to the magic words which had power to stop the bleeding from a wound: "This is blood, that flowed from a piece of wood".

His idea in citing this example was to show that the singer's faith in the power of words should be so enormous that he should be capable of *believing* that a piece of dry wood could bleed, could shed warm, red blood—wood, the driest thing there is.

The Uncertain Life—Padloq (page 95)
Padloq and I often made excursions together, and on one of our many journeys an event occurred which showed him in such a characteristic light that I include the story here. It happened during a walrus hunt on the edge of the ice, out in Frozen Strait.

Padloq might fairly be said to be of a humble, religious turn of mind, that it was his firm belief that all the little happenings of everyday life, good or bad, were the outcome of activity on the part of mysterious powers. Human beings were powerless in the grasp of a mighty fate, and only by the most ingenious system of taboo, with propitiatory rites and sacrifices, could the balance of life be maintained. Owing to the ignorance or imprudence of men and women, life was full of contrary happenings, and the intervention of the angákut was therefore a necessity. Padloq himself was always most concerned about his adopted child, Qahitsoq, on which he and Takornâq alike lavished all their affection. The poor, emaciated creature, a boy, seemed hardly capable of life, and despite all the efforts of Takornâq to feed him and fatten him, with constant meals of seal-meat soup and blubber from her own mouth, he was always whining, even in sleep. Padloq himself once said of the poor little weakling—which after all lacked nothing but its own mother's milk—that "he was as a guest among the living". By way of linking him more strongly to life, they had him betrothed to a fine healthy little girl, who was, like himself, less than a year old. But all efforts were unavailing, the boy died ere the winter was out. During his lifetime, however, the little fellow had furnished material for many conversations, and in the course of these talks with Padloq I could not but think, many a time, how unjust it is to accuse primitive peoples of being only concerned with their food and how to get it with least trouble. True, they say themselves that a man's only business is to procure food and clothing, and while fulfilling his duties in this respect he finds, in his hunting and adventures, the most wonderful experiences of his life. Nevertheless, men may be to the highest degree interested in spiritual things; and I am thinking here not only of their songs and poems, their festivals when strangers come to their place, but also of the manner in which they regard religious questions, wherein they evince great adaptability and versatility. This it is which always gives their accounts that delightful originality which is the peculiar property of those whose theories are based on experience of life itself. Their naturalness makes of them philosophers and poets unawares, and their simple and primitive orthodoxy gives to their presentment of a subject the childlike charm which makes even the mystic element seem credible.

One evening, Padloq, who was an enthusiastic angákoq, had been particularly occupied in studying the fate of the child. We were lying on the bench, enjoying our evening rest, but Padloq stood upright, with closed eyes, over by the window of the hut. He stood like that for hours, chanting a magic song with many incomprehensible words. But the constant repetition, and the timid earnestness of his utterance, made the song as it were an expression of the frailty of human life and man's helplessness in face of its mystery. Then suddenly, after hours of this searching in the depths of the spirit, he seemed to have found what he sought; for he clapped his hands together and blew upon them, washing them, as it were, in fresh human breath, and cried out:

"Here it is! Here it is!"

We gave the customary response:

"Thanks, thanks! You have it."

Padloq now came over to us and explained that Qahîtsoq had been out in a boat the previous summer, the sail of which had belonged to a man now dead. A breeze from the land of the dead had touched the child, and now came the sickness. Yes, this was the cause of the sickness: Qahîtsoq had touched something which had been in contact with death, and the child was yearning now away from its living kind to the land of the dead.

We settled down then all together on the bench, waiting for the meal that was cooking. It was midwinter, the days were short, and the evenings long. A blubber lamp was used for the cooking, the pot being hung over it by a thong from a harpoon stuck into the wall. Suddenly the pot gave a jump, and rocked to and fro, as if someone had knocked it. The heat had melted the snow at the spot where the harpoon was fixed, the harpoon had slipped down a little, jerking the thong, and making the lumps of meat hop in their soup. Padloq, still under the influence of his trance, leapt up from his place and declared that we must at once shift camp, and move up on to the firm old winter ice; for our hut here was built among some pressure ridges forming a fringe between the old ice and the open sea. We had taken up this position in order better to observe the movements of the walrus, but Padloq now asserted that we were too near the open sea, and were filling the feeding grounds of the walrus with our own undesirable emanations. They did not like the smell of us. And the sea spirit Takánakapsâluk was annoyed, and had just shown her resentment by making our meat come alive in the pot. This is said to be a sign often given to people out near the fringe of the ice, and we were obliged to accept it. But the rest of us were not at all inclined to turn out just as that moment, all in the dark, and shift camp. It would be several hours before we got into new quarters, and hours again before we got anything to eat. Therefore, despite Padloq's protest, we stayed where we were, and when we had eaten our fill, crept into our sleeping bags. None of us dreamed how nearly Padloq had been right until next morning, when to our horror we found a crack right across the floor. It was only a narrow one, but wide enough for the salt water to come gurgling up through it now and again. The roof of the hut was all awry over by the entrance, and on knocking out a block of snow, we saw the black waters of the open sea right in front of us. The young ice on which the snow hut was built had broken away, but instead of being carried out to sea, it had drifted in at the last moment among some high pressure ridges kept in place by a small island.

After that I was obliged to promise Padloq that I would in future have more respect for his predictions as a shaman, should we again be out hunting on the ice-edge; for, as Padloq put it, the spirits can, at times, speak through some poor ignorant fellow otherwise of no account, and that to such purpose that even those far wiser may be well advised to heed what is said.

But before a shaman attains the stage at which any helping spirit would think it worth while to come to him, he must, by struggle and toil and concentration of thought, acquire for himself yet another great and inexplicable power: *he must be able to see himself as a skeleton*. Though no shaman can explain to himself how and why, he can, by the power his brain derives from the supernatural, as it were by thought alone, divest his body of its flesh and blood, so that nothing remains but his bones. And he must then name all the parts of his body, mention every single bone by name; and in so doing, he must not use ordinary human speech, but only the special and sacred shaman's language which he has learned from his instructor. By thus seeing himself naked, altogether freed from the perishable and transient flesh and blood, he consecrates himself, in the sacred tongue of the shamans, to his great task, through that part of his body which will longest withstand the action of sun, wind and weather, after he is dead.

As soon as a young man has become a shaman, he must have a special shaman's belt as a sign of his dignity. This consists of a strip of hide to which are attached many fringes of caribou skin, and these are fastened on by all the people he knows, as many as he can get; to the fringes are added small carvings, human figures made of bone, fishes, harpoons; all these must be gifts, and the givers then believe that the shaman's helping spirits will always be able to recognise them by their gifts, and will never do them any harm.

A man who has just become a shaman must for a whole year refrain from the following:

He must not eat the marrow, breast, entrails, head or tongue of any beasts; the meat he eats must be raw, clean flesh. Women during the first year are subject to even further restrictions, but the most important of all is that they are not allowed to sew a single stitch throughout that year.

The last thing a shaman learns of all the knowledge he is obliged to acquire, is the recitation of magic prayers or the murmuring of magic songs, which can heal the sick, bring good weather or good hunting. One can practise magic words simply by walking up and down the floor of one's house and talking to oneself. But the best magic words are those which come to one in an inexpicable manner when one is alone out among the mountains. These are always the most powerful in their effects. The power of solitude is great and beyond understanding. Here is a method of learning an effective magic prayer:

When one sees a raven fly past, one must follow it and keep on pursuing until one has caught it. If one shoots it with bow and arrow, one must run up to it the moment it falls to the ground, and standing over the bird as it flutters about in pain and fear, say out loud all that one intends to do, and mention everything that occupies the mind. The dying raven gives power to words and thoughts. The following magic words, which had great vitalising power, were obtained by Angutingmarik in the manner above stated:

> nunamasuk
> nunʌrzuamasuk
> uḃva mak·ua—
> saunɛrʒuit silʌʒu·p
> qʌqitɔrai—
> pʌrqitɔrai—
> he—he—he.

> tɔ·ʳŋʳʌ·rzuk
> tɔ·ʳŋʳʌ·rzuk
> udludlo
> avatiŋnut
> audlʌrit
> patqɛrnɔgit
> uʷai—uʷai—uʷai!

Angutingmarik was Padloq's father. Peter Freuchen, a member of Rasmussen's expedition, quotes this song in his *Book of the Eskimo*, and says of it: ". . . Padloq, who sang it, said that his father had composed it. One day the father had shot a raven, and while he was contemplating its death agony he had recited the song. The words had come by themselves. But Padloq characterised his father as a man who liked loneliness, a description which—in Eskimo language—is no doubt equivalent to the man's being a poet or angakok (shaman)."

Greeting to the Women of the Feasting House—Orulo (p. 28)
(Orula was the informant; this was a traditional song)
Another festival, only celebrated when there are many people, is
called quluŋᴇrtut. It opens with a challenge between two iglɔre·k,
first to all manner of contests out in the open, and ending with a
song contest in the qag·e. The two rivals, each with a knife, embrace
and kiss each other as they meet. The women are then divided into
two parties. One party has to sing a song, a long, long song which
they keep on repeating; meantime, the other group stand with up-
lifted arms waving gulls' wings, the object being to see which side
can hold out the longer. Here is a fragment of the song that is sung
on that occasion:

> Women, women,
> young, women!
> Aj, they come,
> in fine new furs,
> women, women,
> young women, etc.

The women of the losing party then had to "stride" over to the
others, who surrounded them in a circle, when the men had to try
to kiss them.

After this game an archery contest was held. A target was set up
on a long pole, and the one who first made ten hits was counted the
winner. Then came ball games and fierce boxing bouts. In these, it
was permissible to soften the effect of the blows by wearing a fur
mitten with the fur inside. The combatants had to strike each other
first on the shoulders, then in the eyes or on the temples, and in spite
of the glove, it was not unusual for a collarbone to be broken, or for
a blow in the face to do serious damage. I have at any rate seen a
man who had had one eye knocked out in the course of one of these
tests of strength and manliness. After all these sporting events,
which in the respective games required the two iglɔre·k to be un-
ceasingly up to the mark and to show themselves at their very best,
the conclusion took place in the qag·e, where the two rivals had
again to finish off their duel by a song contest lasting as a rule the
whole night.

Dancing Song—Tutlik (p. 29)
Tutlik and her husband, the shaman Unaleq, travelled to meet Ras-
mussen in the Iglulik village where he was staying in the winter of

1921. They were in a state of near starvation, and in return for some demonstrations of Unaleq's art, Rasmussen supplied them with enough caribou and walrus meat to satisfy their immediate needs:

Tuglik [*sic*] who, unaffected by all minor failings, was a blind admirer of her husband's art, now proposed that we should finish up the evening by playing children's games. She was anxious that I should forget all about her husband's passing weakness as soon as possible, and like a wise woman, chose an old dance song. She had long since discovered that when I touched on the question of Unaleq's relations with the spirits, it was always more self-interest than faith. But she knew that I was very fond of songs and stories, which they themselves did not rank so high as gifts of the spirits. So she drew forth a couple of little girls, little bundles of skins with ruddy cheeks, and placed them one opposite the other. Then, as soon as she started the song, which was sung at a breathless rate which left her gasping, the little girls joined in, crouching down and hopping with bent knees in time to the music. . . .

Report of the Fifth Thule Expedition, Vol. 7, Ch. 1

This (song) also must be heard to produce the full effect; it needs the clear children's voices to give it at its best. The description of the evil days of dearth could not be more intensely given than in the second and sixth verses . . .

The hallucinations which almost invariably accompany actual starvation are then given . . . where things of solid earth become but as a floating mirage to those whose entrails are racked with emptiness . . . And then finally comes the joyous vision of food. . . .

This little song . . . is nothing but a scrap of nursery rhyme, known to all children at play, yet it shows to the full the high level of Eskimo poetry.

Report of the Fifth Thule Expedition, Vol. 7, Ch. 10

Reindeer—Aua (p. 59)

I once went out to Aua's hunting quarters on the ice outside Lyon Inlet to spend some time with the men I have referred to in the foregoing. For several evenings we had discussed rules of life and taboo customs without getting beyond a long and circumstantial statement of all that was permitted and all that was forbidden. Everyone knew precisely what had to be done in any given situation, but whenever I put in my query: "Why?", they could give no answer. They regarded it, and very rightly, as unreasonable that I should require not only an account, but also a justification, of their religious principles. They had of course no idea that all my questions, now that I had obtained the information I wished for, were only intended to make them react in such a manner that they should, excited by my inquisitiveness, be able to give an inspired explanation. Aua had as usual been the spokesman, and as he was still unable to answer my questions, he rose to his feet, and as if seized by a sudden impulse, invited me to go outside with him.

It had been an unusually rough day, and as we had plenty of meat after the successful hunting of the past few days, I had asked my host to stay at home so that we could get some work done together. The brief daylight had given place to the half-light of the afternoon, but as the moon was up, one could still see some distance. Ragged white clouds raced across the sky, and when a gust of wind came tearing over the ground, our eyes and mouths were filled with snow. Aua looked me full in the face, and pointing out over the ice, where the snow was being lashed about in waves by the wind, he said:

"In order to hunt well and live happily, man must have calm weather. Why this constant succession of blizzards and all this needless hardship for men seeking food for themselves and those they care for? Why? Why?"

We had come out just at the time when the men were returning from their watching at the blowholes on the ice; they came in little groups, bowed forward, toiling along against the wind, which actually forced them now and again to stop, so fierce were the gusts. Not one of them had a seal in tow; their whole day of painful effort and endurance had been in vain.

I could give no answer to Aua's "Why?", but shook my head in silence. He then led me into Kublo's house, which was close beside our own. The small blubber lamp burned with but the faintest flame, giving out no heat whatever; a couple of children crouched, shivering, under a skin rug on the bench.

Aua looked at me again, and said: "Why should it be cold and comfortless in here? Kublo has been out hunting all day, and if he had got a seal, as he deserved, his wife would now be sitting laughing beside her lamp, letting it burn full, without fear of having no blubber left for tomorrow. The place would be warm and bright and cheerful, the children would come out from under their rugs and enjoy life. Why should it not be so? Why?"

I made no answer, and he led me out of the house, into a little snow hut where his sister Natseq lived all by herself because she was ill. She looked thin and worn, and was not even interested in our coming. For several days she had suffered from a malignant cough that seemed to come from far down in the lungs, and it looked as if she had not long to live.

A third time Aua looked at me and said : "Why must people be ill and suffer pain? We are all afraid of illness. Here is this old sister of mine; as far as anyone can see, she has done no evil; she has lived through a long life and given birth to healthy children, and now she must suffer before her days end. Why? Why?"

This ended his demonstration, and we returned to our house, to resume, with the others, the interrupted discussion.

"You see," said Aua. "You are equally unable to give any reason when we ask you why life is as it is. And so it must be. All our customs come from life and turn towards life; we explain nothing, we believe nothing, but in what I have just shown you lies our answer to all you ask.

"We fear the weather spirit of earth, that we must fight against to wrest our food from land and sea. We fear Sila.

"We fear dearth and hunger in the cold snow huts.

"We fear Takánakapsâluk, the great woman down at the bottom of the sea, that rules over all the beasts of the sea.

"We fear the sickness that we meet with daily all around us; not death, but the suffering. We fear the evil spirits of life, those of the air, of the sea and the earth, that can help wicked shamans to harm their fellow men.

"We fear the souls of dead human beings and of the animals we have killed.

"Therefore it is that our fathers have inherited from their fathers all the old rules of life which are based on the experience and wisdom of generations. We do not know how, we cannot say why, but we keep those rules in order that we may live untroubled. And so ignorant are we in spite of all our shamans, that we fear everything unfamiliar. We fear what we see about us, and we fear all the invisible things that are likewise about us, all that we have heard of in our forefathers' stories and myths. Therefore we have our customs, which are not the same as those of the white men, the white men who live in another land and have need of other ways."

That was Aua's explanation; he was, as always, clear in his line of thought, and with a remarkable power of expressing what he meant. He was silent then, and as I did not at once resume the conversation, his younger brother Ivaluardjuk took up the theme, and said :

"The greatest peril of life lies in the fact that human food consists entirely of souls.

"All the creatures that we have to kill and eat, all those that we have to strike down and destroy to make clothes for ourselves, have souls, like we have, souls that do not perish with the body, and which must therefore be propitiated lest they should revenge themselves on us for taking away their bodies."

"In the old days, it was far worse than it is now," put in Anarqâq, "Everything was more difficult, and our customs accordingly much more strict. In those days, men hunted only with bow and arrow and knew nothing of the white men's fire-arms. It was far more difficult to live then, and often men could not get food enough. The caribou were hunted in kayaks at the crossing of rivers and lakes, being driven out into the water where they could be easily overtaken in a kayak. But it was hard to make them run the way one wished, and therefore rules were very strict about those places. No woman was allowed to work there, no bone of any animal might be be broken, no brain or marrow eaten. To do so would be an insult to the souls of the caribou, and was punished by death or disaster. . . .

Another song was even more fragmentary, the text being spun out into incessant repetitions, with the customary refrain of aja¹ja: in its original form, as Aua sang it for me the first time, it ran as follows:

Reindeer
aja¹ja¹ja aja aja¹ja¹ja aja
misikʃa¹giga
ajaja¹ja aja
ajaja¹ja aja
natɛrnʌrmiutʌq
ajaja¹ja aja
misikʃa¹gigale
ajaja¹ja aja
pɛraläktik·iga·
ajaja¹ja.

All unexpected I came and took by surprise
The heedless dweller of the plains,
All unexpected I came and took by surprise
The heedless dweller of the plains,
And I scattered the herd
In headlong flight.

I now begged Aua to give me the song in detail . . . .
(Translation, page 59)

Walrus, Aua (page 61)
Some poems are so fashioned that they can be reproduced without difficulty, almost word for word, as they are recited and sung. Such

are the songs I have quoted here and there in the foregoing. But there are others which presuppose a thorough acquaintance with the events described or referred to, and would thus be untranslatable without commentaries that would altogether spoil the effect. This applies more especially to hunting songs, where the animals are not mentioned by name, but indicated by some descriptive phrase, and where various details are explained beforehand, apart from the text proper, the latter being then often rather a kind of encouraging refrain, an incitement to the chorus, who, once in the grip of the tune, simply shout out the words among the other singers, and thus make the singing more pleasing and effective. In such cases, I have been obliged to seek explanatory information from the composers, who then interpreted the text for me into ordinary language, so that it was possible to translate it. I give here some examples of such songs, which would have been the merest guesswork in translation, if the poet himself had not furnished the needful commentary. All these songs are by Aua.

Walrus hunting
ajaja¹ja aja aja¹ja
ajaja¹ja aja aja¹ja
ajaja¹ja aja aja¹ja
tupaguatᴀrivuɳa
imᴀq man·a
sailᴇrata·talᴇrmät
ajaja¹ja aja aja¹ja
ajaja¹ja aja aja¹ja
ajaja¹ja aja aja¹ja
tautuɳ·uᴀrpäk·iga
nap·ᴀriᴀratatlᴀrmät
(aiwᴇq una)
kauligjuᴀq una
ajaja¹ja aja aja¹ja
ajaja¹ja aja aja¹ja
ajaja¹ja aja aja¹ja
tuɳnᴇriʃuɳᴀrivᴀra
tu·ᵛkaᵛnik
ajaja¹ja aja aja¹ja
ajaja¹ja aja aja¹ja
tautuɳ·uᴀrpäk·iga
avatᴀra sᴇrqisᴀ·ratätlarmät
tautuɳ·uᴀrpäk·iga
ajäp·ᴇriᴀriätlarmät
ajaja¹ja aja aja¹ja

138

ajaja¹ja aja aja¹ja
ajaja¹ja aja aja¹ja
tulɔrsa·talɛrmago
aksɔruku·tA·rpAra
(awiŋakuluŋmik
pit·ɔrqutɛqalA·rmän)
ajaja¹ja aja aja¹ja
ajaja¹ja aja aja¹ja
tArqatigigamiuk ima
tuŋnɛriʃuŋArivAra
aŋuwik·aᵛnikle·
ajaja¹ja aja aja¹ja
ajaja¹ja aja aja¹ja
anɛrsA·qArpäm·ata
avaklivun piʒamiŋnik
ajaja¹ja aja aja¹ja
ajaja¹ja aja aja¹ja
ajaja¹ja aja aja¹ja

This hunting song can, however, be directly translated without comment beyond the two parenthetical passages inserted by Aua out of consideration for "the white men". The first of these passages merely indicates that the object of the chase was a walrus, which, he states, need not have been explained to his fellow-countrymen, as it would be apparent from the song itself. The second interpolation tells us that the amulet belonging to the hunting float was a lemming: this explanation likewise would be superfluous to an Eskimo audience, as a lemming is the regular amulet for hunting floats. The translation then runs as follows (see page 61), save that the refrain ajaja¹ja aja aja¹ja, incessantly repeated for the sake of the melody, and otherwise only chosen as easily vocalised words, is here omitted. These words alone however, can work up the chorus to full pitch when constantly repeated, and all can join in. And thus general participation, where everyone present can feel, as it were, a part of the song itself, is perhaps what makes it possible for a song festival to go on for many hours without anyone growing tired.

Polar Bear, Aua, page 60
The following song is typical of the indirect method, where the poet takes it for granted that the situation referred to is known in all its details, and therefore contents himself with throwing out a few words to the chorus, who then, steadily repeating a refrain, allow their own imagination to work on the theme. Anyone not

familiar with the underlying idea of this poetic brevity would be quite unable to understand the meaning, and may then, like a well-known whaling captain, otherwise fully acquainted with the language and customs of these people, form the impression that the text is a kind of poetic riddle-me-re.

tautuŋuArpäk·ivAra
nanɔralik
kiglimile·
ajaja¹ja aja aja¹ja
ajaja¹ja aja aja¹ja
Ersisa·ŋ·uäŋ·iŋmät
saŋuniArniniuna
akuŋniŋin·Ariblugo
ajaja¹ja aja aja¹ja
ajaja¹ja aja aja¹ja
tArqatigigamiŋa
tuŋnErʃuŋArivAra
aŋuᵂik·aᵛnikle·
ajaja¹ja aja aja¹ja
ajaja¹ja aja aja¹ja
ErqasuŋArsin·ArpAra
anErsA·qArpäm·ata
avaklivun.

Literally translated, the meaning is as follows:

It chanced that I caught sight of
one wearing the skin of a bear
out in the drifting pack ice.
ajaja¹ja aja aja¹ja
It came not threateningly.
Turning about
was the only thing that seemed to hamper it.
ajaja¹ja aja aja¹ja
It wore out its strength against me,
And I thrust my lance
into its body.
ajaja¹ja aja aja¹ja
ajaja¹ja aja aja¹ja
I call this to mind
Merely because they are ever breathing self-praise,
Those neighbours of ours to the south and to the north.

I asked Aua to give me an explanation of the actual event which forms the theme of this song, and he told the story as follows:

He was out one day hunting walrus with his brother Ivaluardjuk, when they caught sight of a huge bear, a male. It came forward at once to attack them, running at full speed, looking delighted at the prospect of fresh meat, almost like a cheerful dog that comes running up at a gallop, wagging its tail. And so assured did it seem of the inferiority of its prey that it appeared quite annoyed at having to take the trouble of turning when Aua sprang aside. And now commenced a hunt that lasted the whole day. Ivaluardjuk had clambered up to a ridge of ice and was shouting at the top of his voice to frighten the bear away. So swift and fierce was the bear in its movements that Aua was unable to harpoon it, while Aua himself was so agile that the bear could not get at him. At last the great fat bear became so exhausted that it sat down in the snow, growling like a little puppy in a nasty temper. Then Aua ran up and thrust his lance into its heart. Ivaluardjuk stood up on his ridge of ice a little distance from the scene of the combat and waved his arms delightedly. He was so hoarse with shouting that he could no longer speak.

This is the hunting episode of which the song treats. It has been related so often that Aua can make do with but the briefest reference in his text to the course of events. At my request, he filled in the gaps so as to give the action in full, the result being as follows:

> tautuŋuArpäk·ivAra
> nanɔralik
> kiglimile·
> ɛrsisa·ŋ·uäŋ·iŋmät
> qiŋmizut
> unazutut paŋaliŋmaŋa
> qilamik Aqajäktu·tigiumalƀuŋa
> saŋuniArniniuna
> akuŋniŋin·Ariƀluƀlugo
> pikʃilA·rama
> a·makitaujualArpuguk
> uvla·min uʷalimun
> tArquatigigamiŋa
> uŋnɛrisuŋArivAra
> aŋuʷik·amikle·

(Translation, page 60)

141

iii. THE CARIBOU ESKIMOS

[Throughout the text of the songs, the word reindeer has been substituted for caribou, purely for reasons of rhythm.]

IGJUGÂRJUK AND HIS FAMILY

Igjugârjuk . . . was no humbug, and when I think of all the people I have met on the long stretch between Greenland and Siberia, he occupies an outstanding place among all prominent Eskimos. He was wise, independent, intelligent and exercised great authority over his fellow-villagers. He invited us at once into one of his tents and, as the mighty man he was, he naturally had two wives and two tents. The eldest of the wives, Kibgarjuk (the little gnawed-off bone)— she it was who had given rise to the aforementioned massacre[1]— had now been superseded by a younger beauty by name Atqâralâq (the little one who descends to one), and naturally her tent, which was large and elegant in contrast to that of her rival, was the one into which we were now shown.

The privation we had expected to find had long been relieved by prosperity. In front of the little camp lay a heap of unflensed caribou, so many that it was difficult to count them. One understands what a feast it is to these Eskimos when the migration of the caribou begins, for when I expressed my pleasure at all the splendid meat that lay piled up, I was told that only a month before they had all been on the verge of starvation. In spite of endless hunting there had been no game to find, and all the caches from previous hunts had been emptied. Then one of Igjugârjuk's wives, Kibgarjuk, together with a small adoptive son, had left the camp and started out in the snow storm, dragging a little sledge behind them. Her sole equipment was some implements for fishing for salmon. It was still hard winter then and the wind blew almost incessantly, and Kibgarjuk was lost

---

[1] Many years previously, Igjugarjuk had slaughtered Kibkarjuk's entire family after they had refused to allow him to take Kibkarjuk as his wife.

in the blizzard, apparently the certain prey of the pitiless Hila. Her objective was a small lake several days' journey away, where she intended to try to catch salmon trout. This was the very last resort she could think of. They had tried everywhere in the vicinity of Kazan River and all the surrounding lakes, without success. It was as if everything eatable had been taken from man. Without provisions and without sleeping skins Kibgarjuk and the little boy had dragged themselves to the lake, resting as little as possible in snow huts which they built for themselves when they could hold out no longer—snow huts which, if they did give them shelter from the wind, were ice-cold because they had nothing to warm them up. At the very point of complete exhaustion they had come to the little lake that she believed would prove their salvation, because she had dreamed that it contained salmon trout. Her dream was fulfilled. The lake actually was full of big, fat trout, and thus it was that Kibgarjuk had saved the whole village; but their faces still bore distinct traces of the sufferings they had gone through during the past two winter months.

Now, however, everything was changed. Igjugârjuk at once gave orders that a luxurious feast was to be prepared for us, and two big caribou carcases were put over the fire in enormous zinc baths that had been secured at the trading post at Baker Lake. While the meal was being cooked, we fed our dogs, but hardly had we taken the coverings from our sledge loads when our dog-feed, which consisted of walrus meat, gave rise to the utmost perplexity among the people. Walrus meat had never been seen before at Hikoligjuaq and was subject to absolute taboo. Igjugârjuk, however, who on his many journeys had developed a certain subtlety of mind, was content to issue a prohibition against the young men of the place touching the meat and against knives from the camp being employed for cutting it up. We strangers were placed outside the local taboo and were allowed to cut the meat up with our own knives and to feed our dogs. While this was proceeding a young man, Pingorqa was his name, and he had never been down by the coast, came to us and began to make enquiries about the animals of the sea, and when he asked if seals had horns like the caribou, I realised that I was among people who were widely different in their habits from the Eskimos whom I had hitherto known and to whom the hunting of aquatic mammals is a condition of life.

As soon as we had finished feeding the dogs, we unloaded our sledges and moved into a tent which Igjugârjuk with customary munificence placed at our disposal. He added that his wife Kibgarjuk could help us with the cooking and mending of our clothes. But Kibgarjuk,

143

who heard this, at once came to me and said that she would only help us on condition that her husband ate with us, especially when we ate fine, white man's food : she had already noticed that we had both flour and tea. While assuring her that I regarded this as a matter of course, I could not help being astonished at the really faithful love this woman had for her husband. He had murdered all her family, all her nearest and dearest, it made no difference. Since then he had displaced her and taken a younger wife when she became old; nevertheless, she continued to cherish such affection for him that, with her life as the stake, she could go out on a fishing trip that saved the whole village, but first and foremost her husband, from death by starvation. I discovered later that Kibgarjuk's position towards her husband and his new wife was the same as that of an old servant.

Report of the Fifth Thule Expedition, Vol. 7, No. 2, Ch. 2

Song of the Lemming (p. 32)
This is actually a beast fable, and not a song. In *Snehyttens Sange* it is attributed to Atqaralaq, in the *Report of Fifth Thule Expedition*, it is told by Kibkarjuk, Igjugarjug's other wife : "the woman who told this (fable) explained that the song was composed in a special lemming language. The lemmings call the sky the rounded belly . . ."

Work Song—Kibkarjuk (p. 33)
l. 7. "great wolf's beard" : Kibkarjuk here gives a double image; she has to gather moss and dry twigs for fuel, and indicates this by saying that she plucks the earth, in the same way as one would pluck a bird or tear the bristles from a wolf's upper lip . . . In comparing the willow (salix) she is about to pluck with the beard of the big wolf, Kibkarjuk here uses a circumlocution that is of double effect; for the "big wolf" is also the name of her husband's song-cousin; every time she names him it pleases her husband.

Song of the Rejected Woman—Kibkarjuk (p. 35)
An unusual feature of this song is Kibkarjuk's account of her own hunting experience. On the whole there were strict taboos forbidding women to hunt : "the great animals would be offended and go away from our shores if they were hunted by women." However, as women did accompany the men on hunting journeys to keep house for them etc., it's possible that they did more hunting than was generally allowed.

iv. THE NETSILIK ESKIMOS

THE NETSILIK POETS

Orpingalik, a shaman in high esteem, was an interesting man, well at home in the old traditions of his tribe, not only intelligent, but having a fertile wit. As a hunter, he stood high, and from the respect shown him I could see that he was a big man among his people. In fact, I was told later, when I arrived among the Arviligjuarmiut at Pelly Bay, that he was a strong and deadly archer and the quickest kayakman of them all when the reindeer herds were being pursued at the places where they crossed the lakes and rivers. . . .

Before settling down in earnest among the Netsilingmiut it was of great importance for me to know how many they knew of the tales I had already written down among the Iglulingmiut. Thanks to Orpingalik's rapidity of apprehension I was able to go through almost a hundred different tales in the course of a week. In addition he gave me the words of several magic songs, I paying for them with some of those I had from the Iglulingmiut. It was considered that these transactions were quite legitimate, for as they were made through the agency of a white man, they could not, it was thought, offend the spirits. Translating magic words is a most difficult matter, because they often consist of untranslatable compounds of words, or fragments that are supposed to have their strength in their mysteriousness or in the very manner in which the words are coupled together. But as every magic word has its particular mission, it is considered quite immaterial whether it is understood by humans or not—as long as the spirits know what it is one wants, a reindeer, a seal, or maybe a cure for sickness. Nevertheless, Orpingalik's magic words were easier to understand than they usually are. . . .

In communicating them to me Orpingalik uttered them in a whisper, but most distinctly and with emphasis on every word. His speech was slow, often with short pauses between the words. I have endeavoured to show the pauses by means of a new line of verse. [He gave me] some magic words used for the purpose of ensuring a successful hunt to men who are in strange country. When I had received them Orpingalik declared that these secret words we owned in fellowship almost made us brothers. The spirits of life would regard us as one, as it were, and treat us the same if only we observed all the taboo that life required. . . .

But Orpingalik was not alone a famous shaman; he was also a poet. His imagination was a luxuriant one, and he had a very sensitive mind; he was always singing when he had nothing else to do, and he called his songs "comrades in solitude", or he would say that his songs were his breath, so necessary were they to him, to such an extent were they part and parcel of himself . . . (*My Breath*, p. 38) was composed under the influence of a fit of despondency that once came over him when he could not regain his strength and vigour after a long illness. . . .

One day I asked Orpingalik how many songs he actually had composed. He replied:

"How many songs I have I cannot tell you. I keep no count of such things. There are so many occasions in one's life when a joy or a sorrow is felt in such a way that the desire comes to sing; and so I only know that I have many songs. All my being is song, and I sing as I draw breath."

Orpingalik was not the only singer in his village, however. On the whole, song seemed to be indispensable to these people. They sing at all times of the day. The women not only hum their husbands' songs, but some of them are of their own fashioning. Orpingalik taught me one of his wife's songs. He never called her by name, but always "my little sister". They had a son Igsivalitaq (the frost-bitten one); a year or two before this son had murdered a hunting companion in a fit of temper, and now he lived an outlaw in the mountains round Pelly Bay, fearing that the Mounted Police, of whom he had heard tell, would come for him. And so his mother had made the following song (see p. 41) through her sorrow over her son's fate. . . .

Report of the Fifth Thule Expedition, Vol. 8, Ch. 1

One very rarely sees men or women at their work without their humming a song. They all have their songs, both men and women. And sometimes it happens that children, half in play, half in earnest, make up songs and deliver them among playmates when playing song-festivals in a little snow hut they have built themselves. Great pains are taken to put the words together nicely and skilfully so that there is melody in them, while at the same time they are pertinent in expression. A man who wants to compose a song may long walk to and fro in some solitary place, arranging his words while humming a melody which he also has to make up himself.

In the chapter dealing with the first meeting with the Netsiling-miut mention has already been made of how a great hunter, shaman and poet like Orpingalik rated his songs. Not only are they just as necessary to him as his breath, but they are his comrades in loneliness. With Orpingalik, who of all the Netsilingmiut was the most poetic-ally gifted man, I often discussed the significance of song, not merely as a herald of festivity in the qagsge but also as a valve for their sorrows and cares.

In the following I have attempted to reproduce Orpingalik's views of how a song is born in the human mind. His poetic narrative of course was not the product of a single question, but the result of a most intimate conversation which I have recorded summarily, but retaining his own expressions and illustrations.

(For Orpingalik's statement, see p. xxiii.)

Report of the Fifth Thule Expedition, Vol. 8, Ch. 12

My Breath—Orpingalik (p. 38)

l. 31. "that great white one" : Both in speech and poetry, Eskimos refer to animals by means of their characteristics. I.e., the polar bear is "the white", the seal is "the blubbery", the reindeer is "animal with antlers".

l. 48. "fjord-seal . . ." : There were two methods of hunting seal. The commonest was hunting at the breathing-hole, which involved patiently waiting, often for days at a time, until a seal came up to breathe, and then harpooning it. The other method, practised only in the summer months, necessitated crawling up on a seal as it lay asleep on an ice-floe, and harpooning it before it woke. Orpingalik is in fact referring to the first technique. A hunter's share in the meat in any seal he caught was surprisingly little : there were complex rules about how the blubber, meat, skin, etc., were to be divided among the families in the community : "when going out hunting they would never say 'I am going after a seal' ; they would always say 'I am going out to try to get a hunting share'."

"Unaija-unaija" : the refrain connotes melancholy and resignation, just as in Tutlik's dancing song "Aj-ja-japapé" suggests exuberance.

Song of a Mother—Uvlunuaq (p. 41)
Uvlunuaq is Orpingalik's wife.

Lure—Orpingalik
The shaman word for reindeer used here is *kumaruaq*, and it "refers

147

to the fact that when a very large herd of reindeer is moving over the ground they are compared with lice swarming on a scalp!"

". . . it was so great an art to bring down the [caribou] required for food and clothing that all possible consideration was observed in order to propitiate the souls of the animals."

Report of the Fifth Thule Expedition, Vol. 7, Ch. 8

v. THE SONGS OF DERISION

Song of Derision about Wife-Swapping (p. 71)
l. 18 "putting out the lamps with women" : A sexual game, usually involving more than two couples. The lights would be extinguished, and the group of naked men and women would change places, and "choose" their partners in the anonymity of the darkness.

It will be noticed that the practice of wife-swapping referred to in many of these songs was always done by mutual agreement between couples. Although women had little say in the matter as a rule, they were entitled to refuse their husband's friends, and sometimes did. Clandestine adultery was forbidden, as the situation in *Dispute between Women* demonstrates.

Contempt (p. 77)
Both in this poem and in *Challenge*, two shamans are ridiculed for their fraudulence or ineptitude. This was unusual. As Rasmussen notes in *Report of the Fifth Thule Expedition*, Volume 7, Chapter 5 : "Shamans were never humbugs, or persons who did not believe in their own powers; it was also extremely rare to meet with scepticism among the listeners." One reason for this was that however implausible a shaman's performance might seem, it would have been dangerous to appear sceptical in case the shaman did have magic which he could use to punish your disbelief.
l. 59 "The savage sleigh-dog of the moon" : Rasmussen provides no explanation that I can find. Migssuarnianga has obviously made a fool of himself by announcing that one of his dogs comes from the spirit of the moon. The East Greenlanders regarded the moon spirit as "the most terrible of the punishing deities watching over the deeds of men", whereas to the Iglulik, for example, the moon was "the only well-intentioned spirit known", who would drive his dogs across the Land of the Sky to come to the aid of a barren woman. The Iglulik's equivalent to the Greenlanders' terrible spirit of the moon, was Takanaluk, the Mother of the Sea Beasts, who in her

original mortal form was compelled by her father to marry a dog. Takanaluk (or Takánakapsâluk) lived in a house at the bottom of the sea, regulating the amount of game available to man. In times of unsuccessful hunting, a good shaman would "visit" her in her kingdom and request her to provide more game: "In the passage leading to the house lies Takánakakapsâluk's dog stretched across the passage taking up all the room; it lies there gnawing at a bone and snarling. It is dangerous to all who fear it, and only the courageous shaman can pass by it, stepping straight over it as it lies; the dog then knows that the bold visitor is a great shaman, and does him no harm."

Report of the Fifth Thule Expedition, Vol. 7, Ch. 5.

vi. CHARMS (pp. 94–100)

Magic words are addressed either to the spirits of the air or to the souls of departed humans or animals. They can procure the healing of sickness, lay snow storms, or cause game animals to let themselves be killed by a hunter.

Some of them have their own melodies, which are always very monotonous and must be sung slowly. Others, on the other hand, have merely to be spoken in a whisper, but distinctly and repeated again and again.

They are sung or uttered according to subject and purpose, either inside a house in the early morning, before anyone has trodden the floor, or outside in the open air at a place, far from the beaten track, where there are no footprints of man. It is the usual thing that ordinary speech is not employed, but the special language of the shamans. Sometimes they make use of ancient words that have fallen into disuse in daily parlance, or vague and incomprehensible phrases all intended to increase the effect and mysteriousness.

Magic words descend from father to son, but may also be bought for a good price of a shaman. As soon as one has imparted magic words, magic prayers or magic songs to another, they only work for the benefit of the new owner, who must never utter them where others can hear them.

Report of the Fifth Thule Expedition, Vol. 8, Ch. 9.